Laurence King Publishing

World Without Words - Michael Evamy

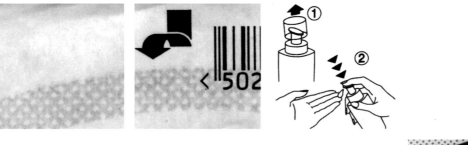

Published in 2003 by Laurence King Publishing Ltd
71 Great Russell Street
London WC1B 3BP
United Kingdom
Tel: +44 20 7430 8850
Fax: +44 20 7430 8880
e-mail: enquiries@laurenceking.co.uk
www.laurenceking.co.uk

A catalogue record for this book is available from the
British Library.

ISBN 1 85669 319 8

Printed in China

World Without Words - Contents

A silent universe

The graphic design in this book is the kind that slips silently by us, all the time, every day. Yet it exerts a special kind of authority over us. In fact, it is the kind of design that could come to form the graphic imprint of our age. It performs a function that is increasingly in demand in our world: that of imparting information without the need for words. World Without Words is about the compression of meaning into non-verbal, purely visual forms, about the delivery of information in ways that satisfy our need for speed, and that transcend individual languages and cultures.

There has never been so much communication that is international and instantaneous, and therefore ill-served by language; there has never been so much energy put into devising graphic alternatives to reading. World Without Words takes a trip through this silent graphic universe. Some of the material here aspires to universal familiarity; some items were never meant to be seen by large audiences. A few were not designed for human consumption at all but for machines or alien life-forms. This is a world without words: a collection of the commonplace, the curious, the enlightened, the misguided, the obvious, the obscure, the systematic, the ad hoc, the high-tech, the low-tech, the local, the national, the global and the universal in graphic communication.

A scream in the desert

At 6.38 p.m. local time on Saturday January 5 2002, a milestone was reached at the Carlsbad Field Office of the US Department of Energy, 20 miles east of the town of Carlsbad, New Mexico. The 28 drums of material coming through the site's main gate on board heavily guarded trucks were the 500th shipment, in all, of 'transuranic waste' from sites across the US, including Los Alamos National Laboratory (also in New Mexico) and Idaho National Engineering and Environmental Laboratory in the north west.

Transuranic waste is the more mundane rubbish created in the manufacture of nuclear weapons: contaminated 'clothing, tools, rags, debris, residues and other non-liquid disposable items', in DoE words. The Carlsbad Field Office is located on top of the Waste Isolation Pilot Plant (WIPP), the place that the US Government chose in the mid-nineties for the 'permanent underground disposal' of America's 'defense-generated radioactive waste'. Consisting of a vast underground repository, or system of vaults, at the bottom of a 660m. deep mineshaft, the WIPP is, essentially, a hole in the ground into which the nation's stockpile of at least 62,000 cubic metres of transuranic waste will eventually descend. That's enough to fill 16 Olympic-sized swimming pools, or provide a coffee cup full of lethally radioactive refuse for every American citizen.

The trouble is, the stuff cannot just be forgotten once it is buried and out of sight. Quite the opposite: what lies beneath this place must always be remembered. People like digging around here – it's just across the

trefoils has escaped and stick man is lying, twig-like, on the ground.

The second panel displays just a single drawing. Three human faces are plotted around a circular line that begins at the three o'clock position and continues anti-clockwise to the seven o'clock position. The first face registers discomfort or disgust, as if there's a bad smell in the air. The second (around the 10 o'clock position) shows no expression, and the final one is beaming with joy. A set of the same trefoil symbols used in the first diagram, descend in size as the circular path is traced, and dotted around the drawing are a star and a number of small circles (see page 29).

What do these silent messages mean? The first one is fairly obvious, given what you now know about the WIPP: it depicts the potentially fatal consequences of digging or drilling in the area. The second would be a total mystery to most people, even today. It displays, we are told, the movement of the celestial north pole relative to various constellations over the next 10,000 years, and offers to a reader familiar with astronomy a method of determining the time since closure of the WIPP.

Would pictures do the job of scaring off seventh millennium visitors? It's a lot to ask of a few cartoon-like panels; in fact, it's hard to think of any instance where this kind of visual narrative has been bestowed with a greater responsibility. And it's hard to envisage our descendants simply taking heed and turning tail. They might understand that their distant, backward ancestors were fearful of this place – but why should they be? The 20th century's breakers and enterers of Pharaohs' tombs hardly set a good example. Four thousand years from now, the trespassers will just start digging, and no number of radiation trefoils will stop them.

Saving seconds

Back in this day and age, however, the WIPP 'markers' make perfect sense. Pictorial signs are considered a form of cross-cultural communication that mankind has refined to an art-form. All the time in our daily lives, we encounter, process and place our trust in non-verbal, graphic information: visual warnings, symbol systems, signs, pictorial instructions, icons, logos, diagrams. Notwithstanding the fact that before the WIPP deposits have lost any of their potency, humans will most likely have developed forms of communication that we cannot begin to foresee, some crude diagrammatic pictures etched on to a metal plate offer our best chance of getting our message across.

As conventional literacy suffers, visual literacy thrives. Thanks to information overload, or more accurately, text overload, attention spans are collapsing. Fewer people are reading books and newspapers; they edit, scan and skim-read. Our appetite for the reading of words has declined, but we have become skilled at reading and recognizing coded images and pictorial representations. Think about the thousands of

(also referred to by its maker as 'A cutting-edge, progressive, advanced, forward-looking, radical, avant-garde, revolutionary new hair care line from Lamaur'). ER, 24, 2DTV, GMTV, SMTV, FAQ, CDUK, TOTP 2 and UBOS – from one week's terrestrial TV schedules in the UK in April 2002.

Strangers to texting might wonder how any kind of personal expression or emotion can be conveyed via strings of bald abbreviations and hacked-about words. It can't. However, developing at a similar rate (despite originating some 20 years ago) via mobile phones and email has been the language of emoticons: pictorial icons constructed of keyboard characters and punctuation marks that indicate the spirit in which a message has been sent.

Visual shorthand of all kinds, new and not-so-new, indulges our taste for haste. And it's not going away: it's too late to slow down. The Internet and email, via ever-faster connections, put us within easy reach of billions of people, organizations, customers, events, goods and services from all over the globe. Globalization is a fact: trade is expanding, tourism is rising and migration is booming. Until the mid-eighties, economic integration was hampered by war, depression, protectionism and restrictions on movement. But now it's all taking off. The unrelenting pressure on businesses and public services is for greater speed. The same volume of international trade as was conducted in the whole of 1949 was carried out in a single day in 2000.

The growth in computing power, as it adds intelligence and speed to the more mundane technologies in consumer products, is driving the speed at which we perform everyday operations – and it is following an exponential curve. Sometime around 2007, claims Intel, it will be building microprocessors containing a billion transistors, running at speeds approaching 20 GHz and operating at less than one volt. Meanwhile, the world's fastest supercomputer (as of August 2001), IBM's ASCI White, is capable of 12.3 million million calculations per second and takes up a space the size of two basketball courts. (What's it for? 'Simulating in three dimensions the aging and operation of nuclear weapons', we are told, and thereby supporting the 'safety and reliability' of the US nuclear stockpile. One wonders whether ASCI White could simulate in 3D the consequences of a violation of the WIPP repository. It might at least lead to some more realistic, and hard-hitting, pictorial warnings.)

All of this processing power is fuelling our appetite for visual shorthand to guide us around daily duties. But it is also leading to new ways of visually displaying data, so that non-experts can quickly gain a holistic grasp of complex phenomena. TV weather forecasts, with their computer-generated projections, are one example. High-quality information graphics on any subject are easily available on the Web. We have become incredibly adept at sifting information, filtering it and ordering it for our own consumption and use. And we retain an instinctive preference for processing information presented to us in a visual, rather than verbal form.

state line from Texas. Somehow, future generations have to be warned of the hazards. And not just future generations, but future civilizations: material of the kind buried at Carlsbad remains dangerously radioactive for many thousands of years.

Displaying a level of care for humanity not normally associated with a manufacturer of weapons of mass destruction, the US government assembled panels of experts to devise a system of markers of different scale that would advertise the site's hidden dangers to future inhabitants, whether friend, foe or alien. A massive earthwork and a series of colossal granite monoliths around the site's perimeter will indicate, Stonehenge-style, that this is a place that held great significance in a previous age. There will be an 'information center' concealed within the earthwork, housing vast volumes of records and data. And there will be 'DANGER' signs and full written explanations engraved in stone in seven languages – the six official United Nations languages (English, French, Spanish, Chinese, Russian and Arabic) and Navajo.

The citizens of New Mexico in 6003 AD might understand every word of what's written in the verbal messages they find. But we certainly can't be sure of that. The languages that we use today may have evolved beyond recognition – as WIPP documents point out, English is almost unrecognizable from the language of Sir Gawain and the Greene Knight (written a mere 625 years ago). Since the 'regulatory time frame' for protecting the site from intruders is 10,000 years and it is not fully known at present how any of these languages might develop or depart from their current form in that time, or even if language itself will survive as a form of communication, it has been deemed necessary to convey the most essential information in purely pictorial terms too.

Here, images or, more accurately, diagrams, are the fall-back option. If they don't get the words, the thinking is, they'll get the pictures. There are two main panels, both still in draft form (the DoE has decades in which to work them up), which will appear on the perimeter monuments at the WIPP. The first one features a series of four line drawings, depicting a sequence of events in which a smiling human stick figure stands by as a hole is dug in the ground. By the third frame, the hole has reached a depth of 0.66km., and a mystery stratum has begun to release back, trefoiled symbols (what you and I know as the accepted symbol for radioactivity). The stick man's face has mutated into that of the figure in Edvard Munch's 'The Scream'. By the final picture, a cloud of

advertising messages our brains are asked to process every day.

We have spent the last 100 years inventing less demanding, less time-consuming alternatives to reading: radio, TV, movies, video games, the Internet and now mobile phones that can take and send pictures. When we're not channel-hopping, surfing or text messaging, we're following the advice, directions and warnings of a million symbols, signs and logotypes. There's a symbol that stands for something everywhere you look. Without them, we'd be lost.

Our lives are accelerating. No one wants to wait any more. Everyone wants quick answers, and manufacturers and service providers are responding with endless ways of saving us precious seconds. Vending machines, microwave ovens, mobile phones and remote controls were just the start. Express checkouts, pizza delivery companies, petrol pumps that allow credit card payment, 'door close' buttons in lifts, high-speed check-ins, drive-thru' fast-food outlets – they all feed our desire to do things faster. And they speak to us through logos, icons, symbols and pictures. Words get in the way, take up too much space, and exclude those who don't speak the 'native' language. Without our ability to understand road signs, computer icons, pictorial instructions, packaging labels, public information symbols, product graphics, newspaper diagrams and charts, our lifestyles would be slower and probably a lot more hazardous.

Language is getting left behind in the rush. You can see words getting trampled underfoot, such is the volume and speed of new communication media. The incredible rise of short message services (SMS), which are helping keep many mobile phone networks afloat, can be put down to the popularity of 'texting' among 12–25 year olds, in which, for speed, messages are peppered with acronyms of everyday slang and abbreviations replacing certain syllables with numbers. www.netlingo.com lists around 350 examples of cybershorthand, from CUL8R (see you later), GAL (get a life) and W/E (whatever), to DYSTSOTT (did you see the size of that thing?) and BBFBBM (body by Fisher, brains by Mattel). Business and the media have been quick to hijack the fashion:
FCUK – a hugely successful rebranding of the French Connection clothing chain
HLND FSTVL – used on posters in The Netherlands advertising the 2002 Holland Festival
XTRMNTR (Exterminator) – a CD by PRML SCRM (Primal Scream)
B IN10SE ('Be Intense') – 'Professional hair stuff 4U'

In the last decade the Internet has upped the stakes massively. The World Wide Web is primarily a visual medium. Michael Schrage, writing in Wired magazine, foresaw as early as 1996 that corporate websites would 'become more comic-like', and predicted 'a shift from language-centric to iconic communication. Just as we have global traffic signs, we'll have global Internet icons.' Six years later, rival operating systems and browsers have become almost indistinguishable and Web icons could follow. Some campaigning organizations have gained invaluable publicity by combining the power of the Internet with website homepages that 'feature 'infographics', statistical maps or other data displays to make their point more eloquently and far more immediately than paragraphs of text. Rolling the mouse over a menu on the homepage of www.scorecard.org, for instance, brings up a succession of maps showing concentrations of air pollution, lead hazards, animal waste from factory farms and other modern ills across the US. Budding Erin Brockoviches can type in their zip code and gain local information on about environmental problems.

The cost of words

Accelerations in technology and the accompanying proliferation of globally available media channels – many of which are US-based – offer an illusion that the world is shrinking and that, before too long, the English language, in a variety of forms, will be adopted as some kind of worldspeak. While that would be convenient for global businesses and brands that currently spend fortunes on translation, the idea of Global English is simply wishful thinking on their part, according to language experts. Most of the world's citizens do not speak any English at all, either as a first, second or third language.

For now, the world's peoples must either be addressed in their own language, or by non-verbal means. Organizations have learned to do the first, and are now feeling 'her way towards the second. Not long ago, some of the world's biggest, most global brands only maintained English-language websites, but now all the big-brand dot com homepages offer links to numerous country sites. It allows those companies to make all kinds of wonderful noises about 'inclusiveness' and a workforce 'rich in its diversity of thinking' (Coca-Cola), but the costs are significant.

Today international businesses are learning the value – and cost efficiencies – of wordlessness. Why bother with all those translations when you could produce just one set of self-assembly furniture instructions, one washing tablet package design or one billboard ad to satisfy all your markets? Hardware manufacturers such as Apple and Hewlett-Packard, faced with the challenge of talking non-techie consumers all over the world through the process of 'Getting Started', have begun to invest in the development of simplified user documents that, beyond the opening page(s), are completely devoid of verbiage, technical or otherwise. Sequences of illustrations guide users through the connections of cables and hardware they need to make, without burdening them with an explanation of what a USB socket is. Meanwhile, Coca-Cola's recent campaign of billboard ads featuring massively inflated details of its red and white logotype could have run anywhere in the world. Having been tongue-tied by translations of its advertising in the past – the name was first translated in China phonetically, as ke-kou-ke-la, a phrase that literally means 'bite the wax tadpole' – this megabrand knows perhaps better than most the linguistic challenges of global empire-building.

What Coca-Cola and many other global organizations are all aware of is that around one in six of the world's population – including 10 million US citizens – must be reached in ways that don't involve words: they cannot read or write. Textless advertising, of which more and more is being produced, and logos whose iconographic status is elevated with each costly makeover, are doing the job, almost incidentally, of speaking to low-literacy consumers. There are also many areas – pharmaceutical packaging, for example – in which verbal instructions might be replaced by pictorial equivalents to make life easier and less hazardous for non-readers. Health advice on contraception and childcare is already produced in comic-book form in some of the world's poorest nations.

With bandwidths increasing – 'satellite Internet' promises download speeds up to 2000 times faster than a 28.8kbps modem – and website design inviting more intuitive, graphic-led interaction, it is possible to envisage a Web that relies a lot less on language. A less wordy Web is inevitable; a wordless Web is a distant possibility. We are starting to see, albeit for experimental, promotional or art-based purposes, examples of wordless websites emerge. These pioneers might offer more mainstream sites valuable lessons in how to lead visitors intuitively around a wordless Web environment. And if ever, as figures such as Robert Reich have suggested, the richest nations should decide to tackle illiteracy by helping to put the world's poorest communities online, then websites with non-verbal navigation could provide a vital introduction to the Internet for non-readers, and a first step on the road to literacy. A few more wordless computer manuals might come in handy, too.

Last words

World Without Words, however, has no such grand scheme in mind. It isn't making any claims about a supremacy of image or symbol over the written word, or that there will be world peace if we all start communicating exclusively in some kind of pictorial esperanto. Some of the developments that have accompanied the advance of our visual culture – the decline of literacy and the drop in attention spans – are regrettable at the very least, but it isn't the place of this book to lament them. Visual languages, symbols, pictorial descriptions – it's not as if these things are new. Iron-age cave-dwellers, Egyptian chroniclers, classical religious painters, German philosophers, comic book illustrators and countless others – known and unknown – have all had an indirect hand in the development of what's in this book. One hundred and twenty years before the Waste Isolation Pilot Plant landed in their backyard, Navajo Indians were recording the arrival of the railroad at Gallup, New Mexico, in dazzling pictorial weavings.

What this book does do is capture the current state of an ancient art: the use of pictures, symbols and graphic systems to convey information. It's an art that is today being stretched like never before to perform extraordinary feats of communication, to the benefit of millions. World Without Words reaches far and wide to capture a sense of this diversity. Chapter One focuses on the silent graphic infrastructure of modern life: the swathe of symbols, applications and systems, conceived in the most part by public authorities or global commercial concerns, that seek to exert control, for better or worse, on our behaviour. Chapter Two reveals the diversity in the details: how the influence of regional and local cultures, and of individuals, can unintentionally subvert and enrich purportedly 'universal' systems. Finally, Chapter Three brings together a wide array of innovations and artistic appropriations that question our acceptance of conventional visual languages or ally established techniques of graphic information to radical causes.

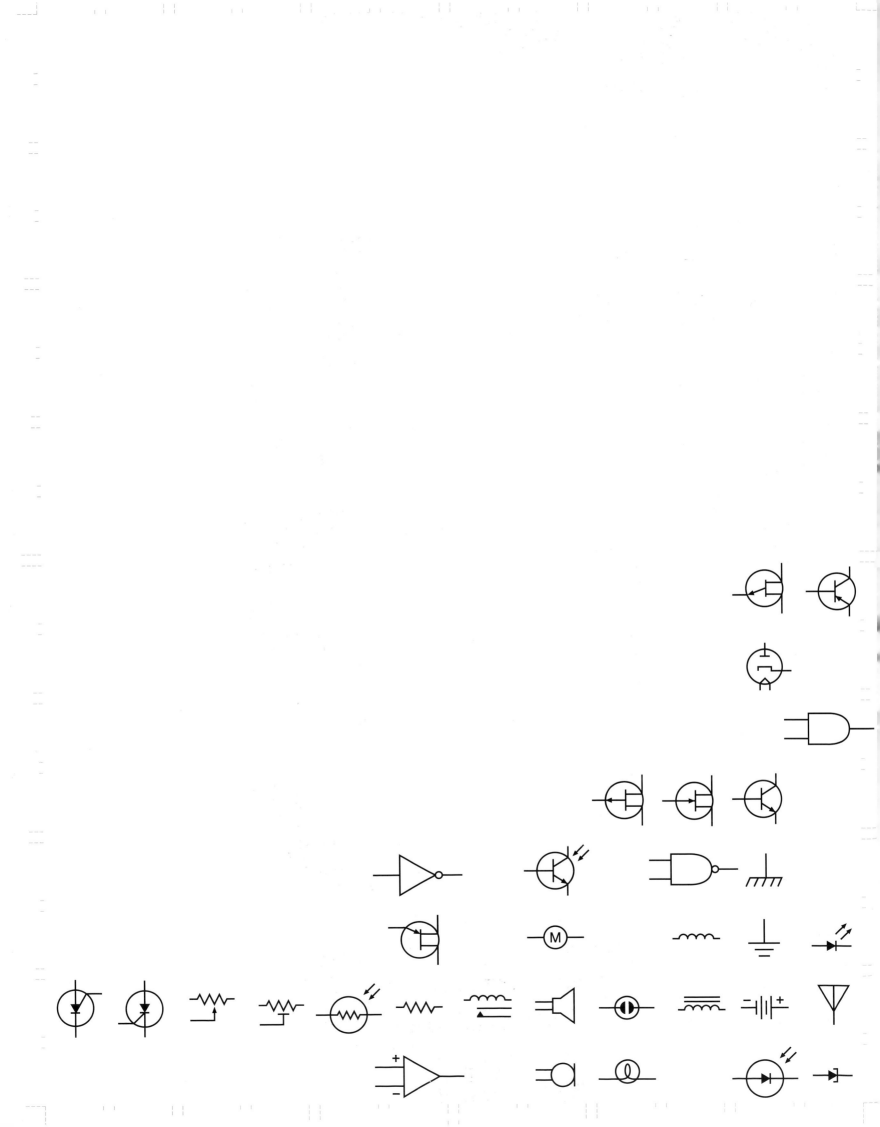

International circuit diagram symbols

Symbols used in specialized branches of engineering and science - usually developed by a process of international technical consultation - are apparently the only kind that have avoided cultural associations and remained 'neutral'. Those used in circuit diagrams, for example, transcend all boundaries and are genuinely "universal".

average of 10 new outlets a month. In many countries, Colonel Sanders is not just a logo but the face of corporate America. In Muslim Pakistan, following US bombing of Afghanistan in October 2001, his features were the first target of protestors.

→ WORDS

KFC visual identity

US megabrands now measure annual growth in their home market in low single digits. If they want to grow faster, they have to go global. KFC is typical. The chain has 5400 US 'restaurants' and 6400 overseas, in 85 countries. 736 million KFC chickens are consumed each year in the world. Laid head to claw, these birds would encircle Earth at the equator 8.5 times. In China, where it is now the most recognized foreign brand, even though a value meal costs the equivalent of the average person's wages for six hours' work, KFC is opening an

KFC: Colonel Sanders
International circuit diagram symbols

→ WORDS

PIC0001
PIC0002

016
017

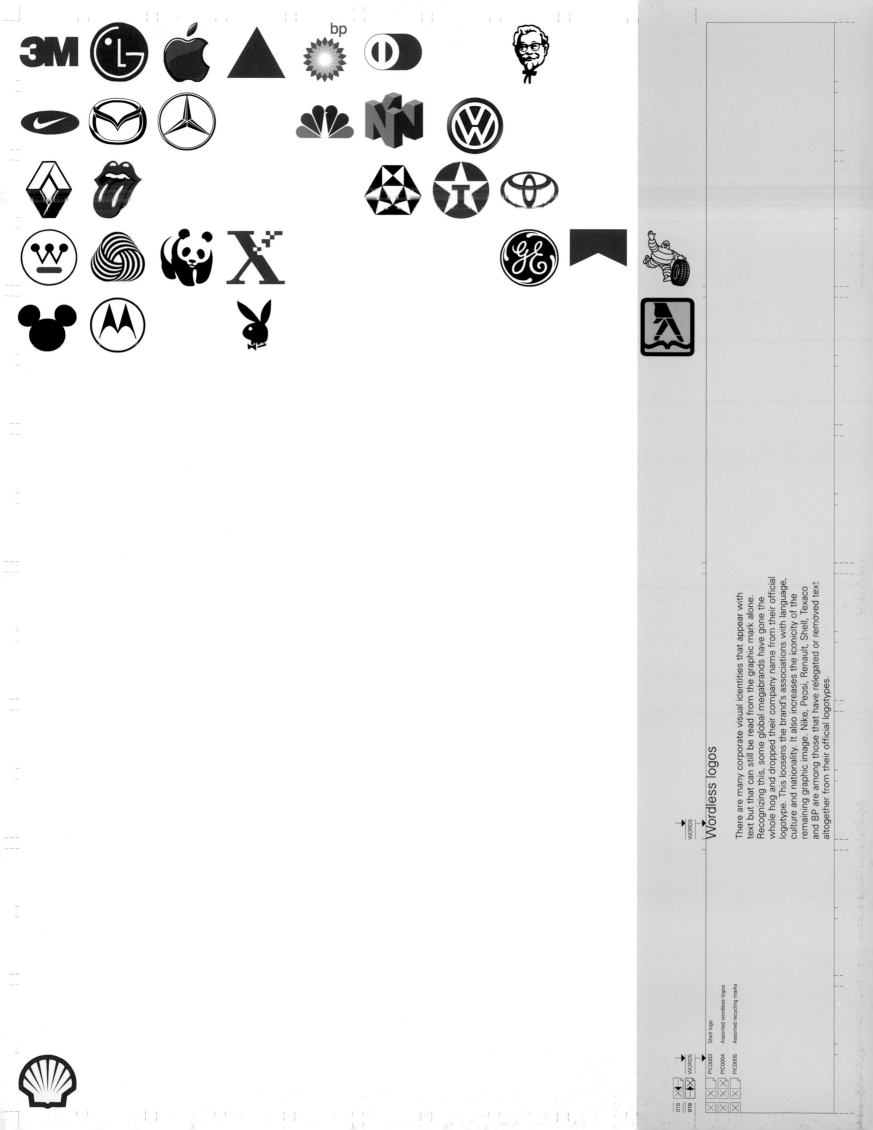

Wordless logos

There are many corporate visual identities that appear with text but that can still be read from the graphic mark alone. Recognizing this, some global megabrands have gone the whole hog and dropped their company name from their official logotype. This loosens the brand's associations with language, culture and nationality. It also increases the iconicity of the remaining graphic image. Nike, Pepsi, Renault, Shell, Texaco and BP are among those that have relegated or removed text altogether from their official logotypes.

WORDS

PIC0003 Shell logo
PIC0004 Assorted wordless logos
PIC0005 Assorted recycling marks

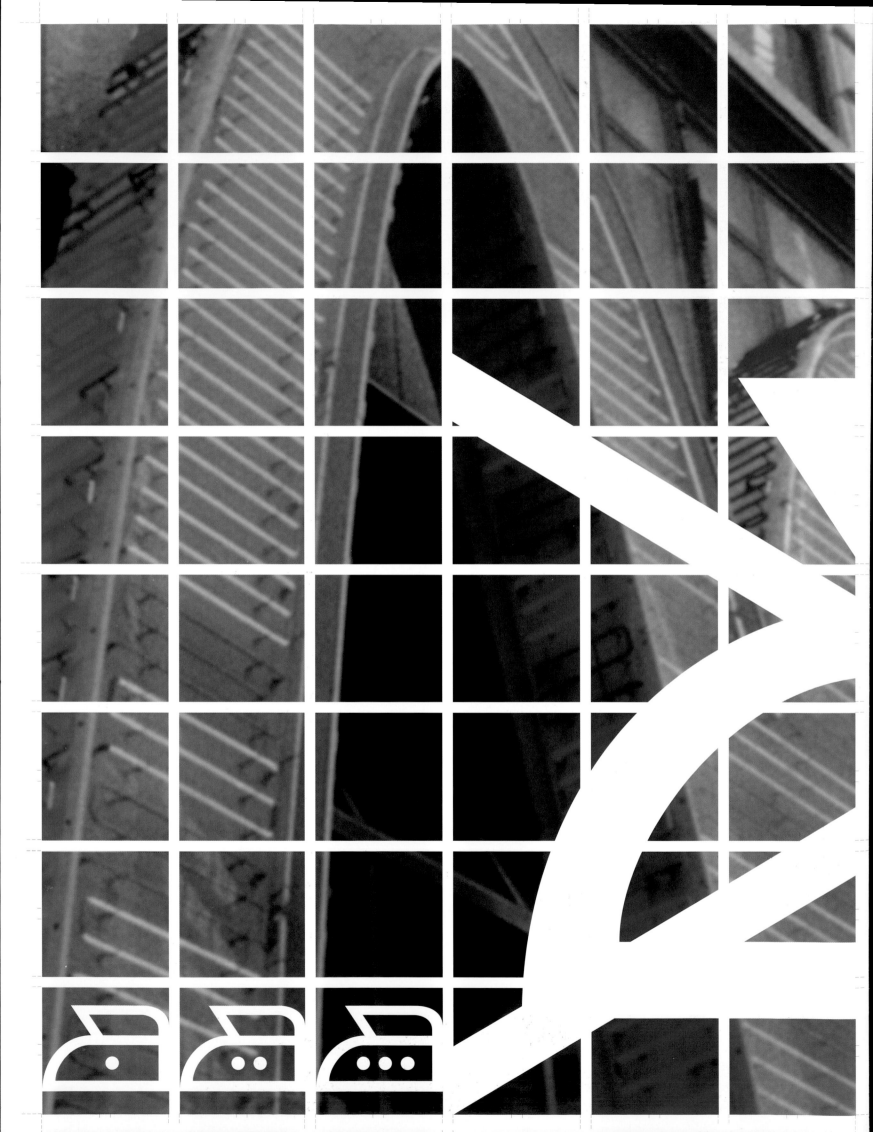

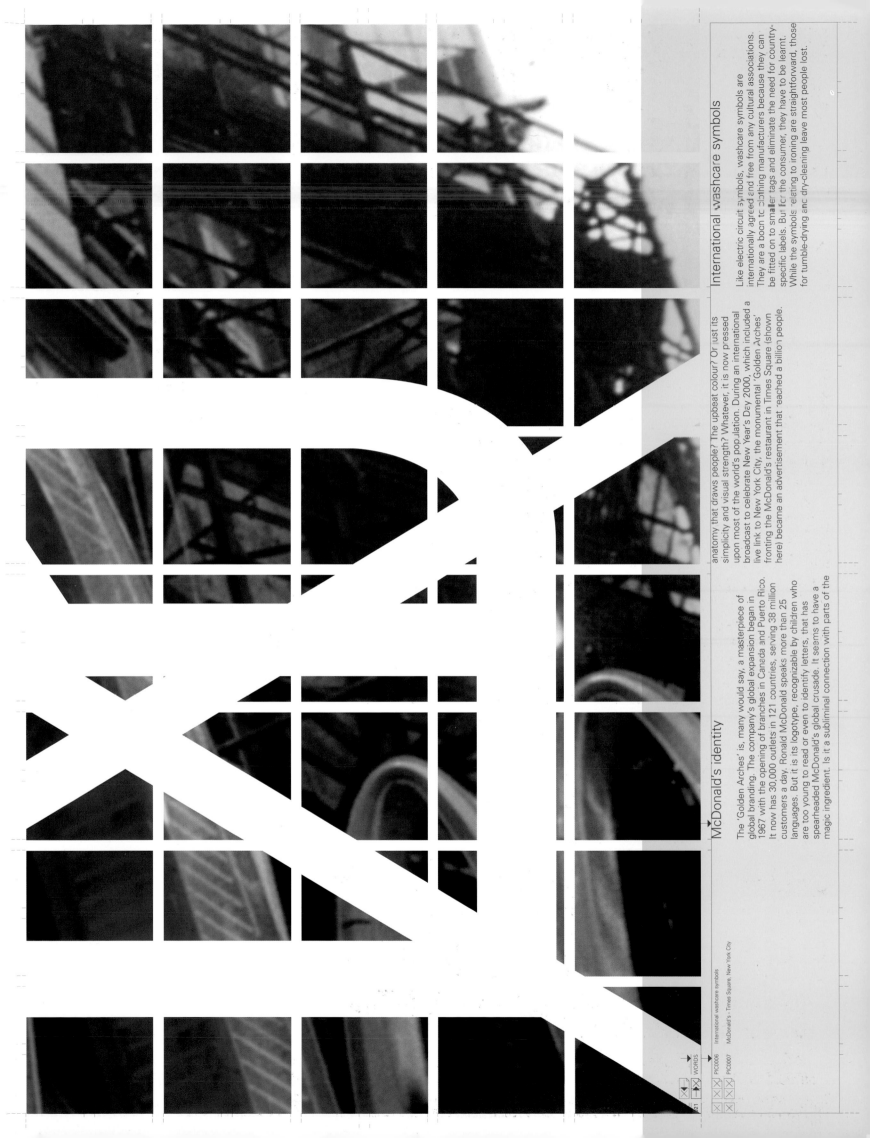

International washcare symbols

Like electric circuit symbols, washcare symbols are internationally agreed and free from any cultural associations. They are a boon to clothing manufacturers because they can be fitted on to smaller tags and eliminate the need for country-specific labels. But for the consumer, they have to be learnt. While the symbols relating to ironing are straightforward, those for tumble-drying and dry-cleaning leave most people lost.

anatomy that draws people? The upbeat colour? Or just its simplicity and visual strength? Whatever, it is now pressed upon most of the world's population. During an international broadcast to celebrate New Year's Day 2000, which included a live link to New York City, the monumental 'Golden Arches' fronting the McDonald's restaurant in Times Square (shown here) became an advertisement that reached a billion people.

McDonald's identity

The 'Golden Arches' is, many would say, a masterpiece of global branding. The company's global expansion began in 1967 with the opening of branches in Canada and Puerto Rico. It now has 30,000 outlets in 121 countries, serving 38 million customers a day. Ronald McDonald speaks more than 25 languages. But it is its logotype, recognizable by children who are too young to read or even to identify letters, that has spearheaded McDonald's global crusade. It seems to have a magic ingredient. Is it a subliminal connection with parts of the

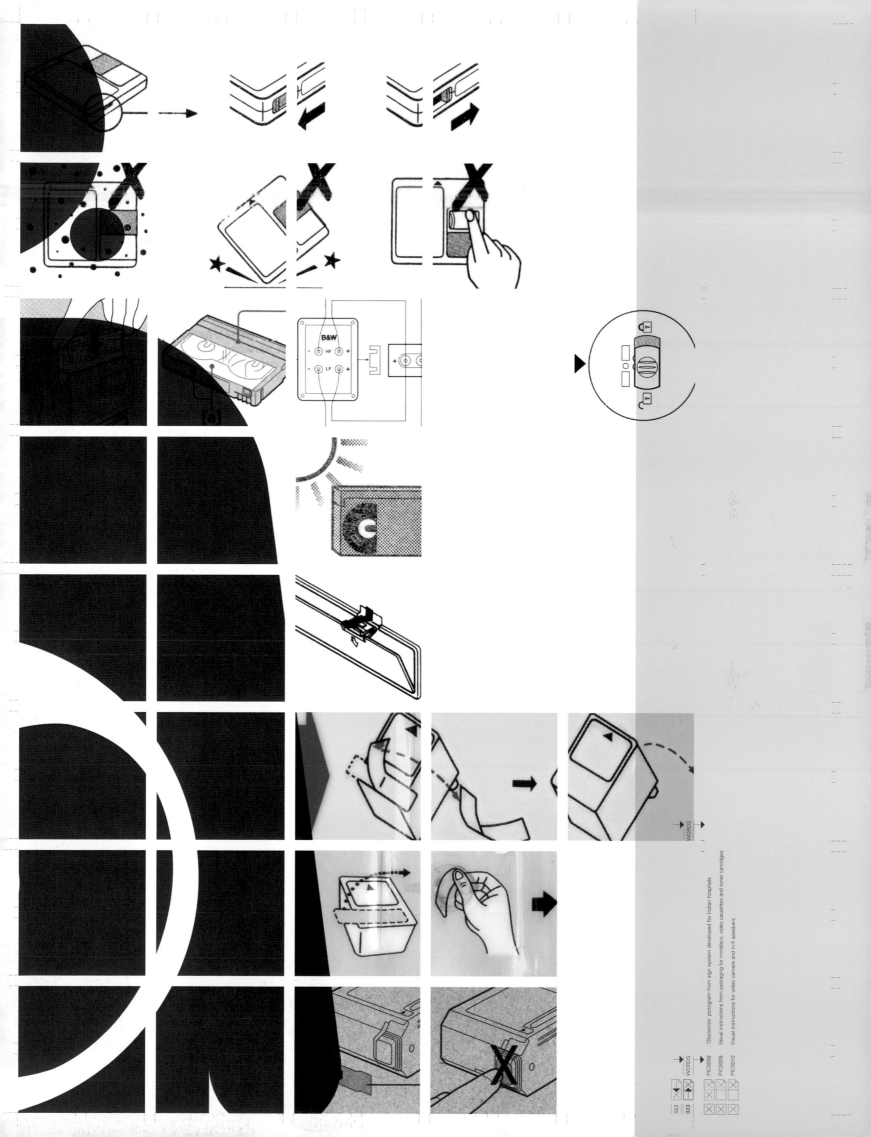

'Obstetrics' pictogram from sign system developed for Indian hospitals

PIC0008   Visual instructions from packaging for minidisc, video cassettes and toner cartridges

PIC0009

PIC0010   Visual instructions for video camera and hi-fi speakers

WORDS

022
023

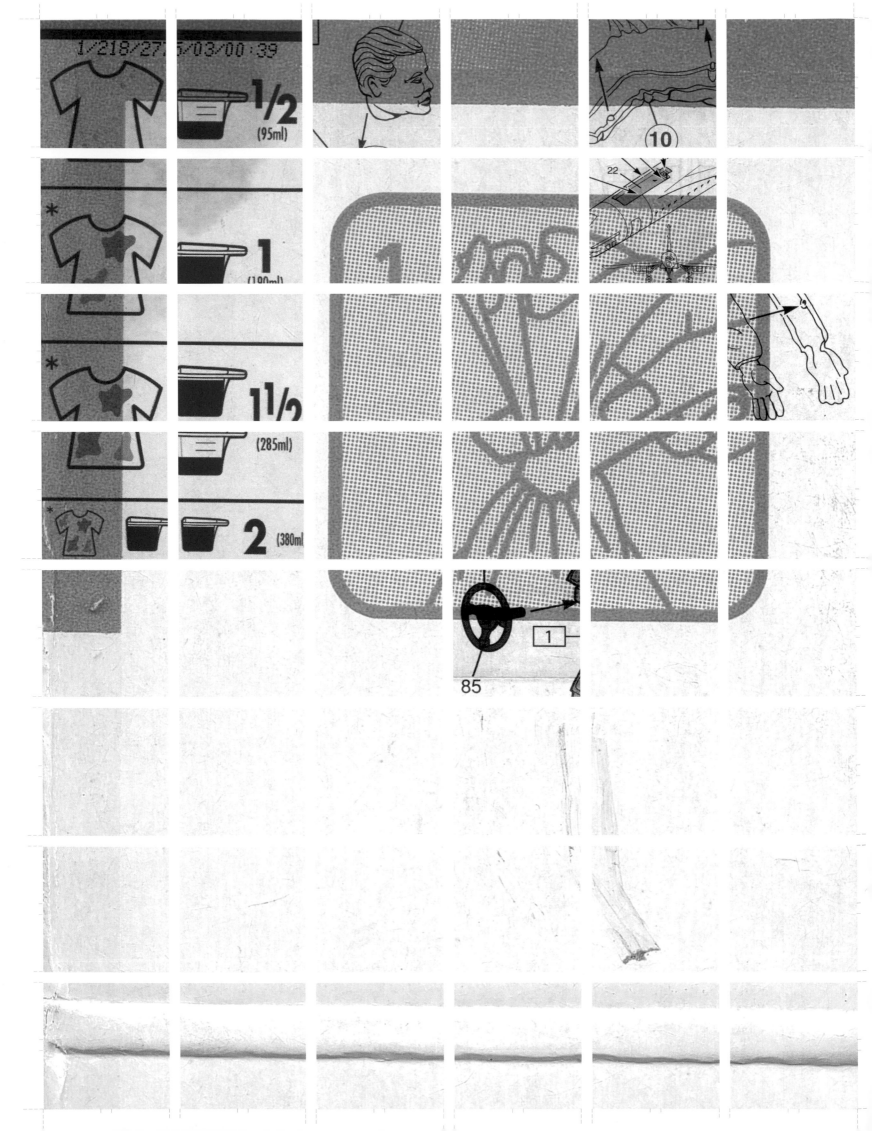

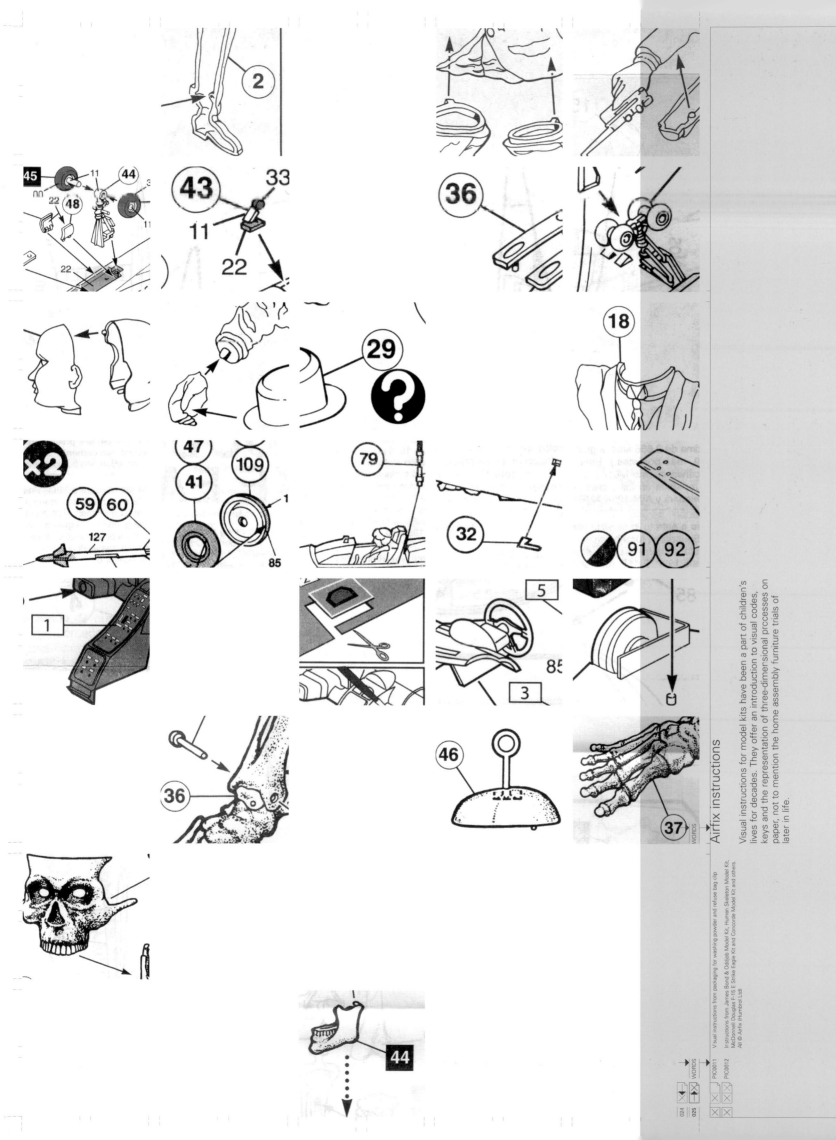

Airfix instructions

Visual instructions for model kits have been a part of children's lives for decades. They offer an introduction to visual codes, keys and the representation of three-dimensional processes on paper, not to mention the home assembly furniture trials of later in life.

Visual instructions from packaging for washing powder and refuse bag clip

Instructions from James Bond & Oddjob Model Kit, Human Skeleton Model Kit, McDonnell Douglas F-15 E Strike Eagle Kit and Concorde Model Kit and others.
All © Airfix (Humbrol Ltd)

PIC0011
PIC0012

WORDS

024
025

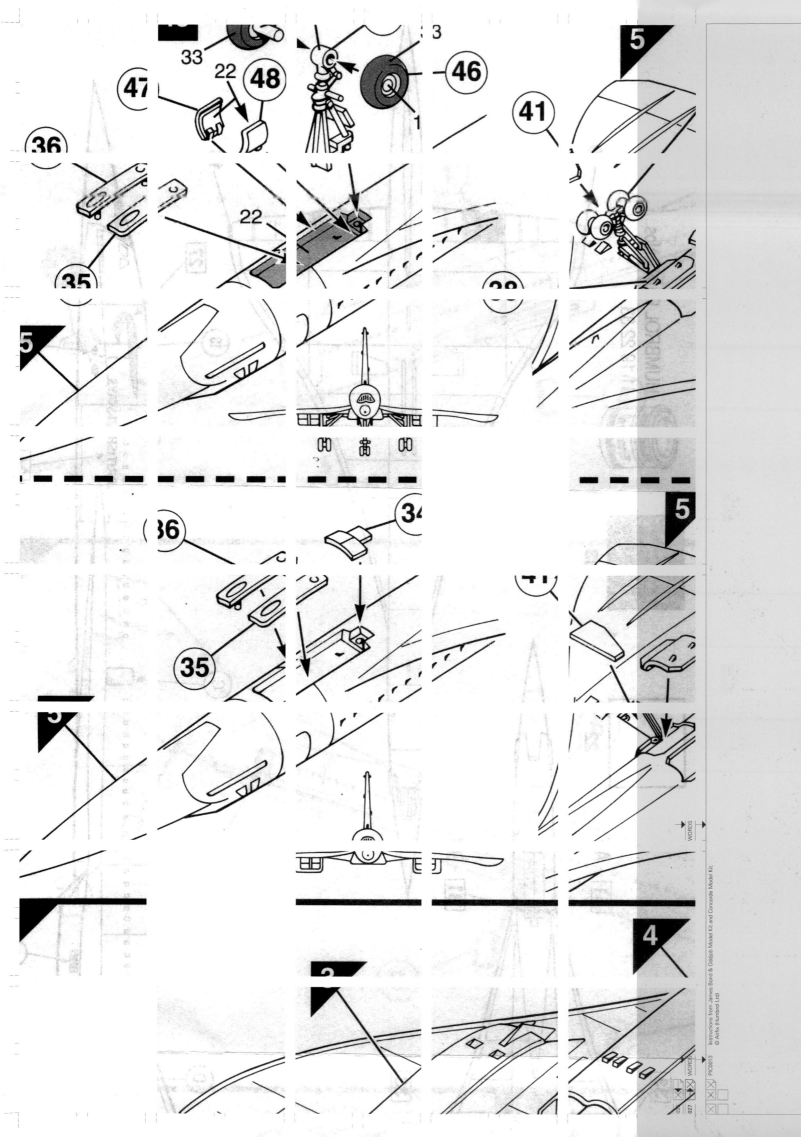

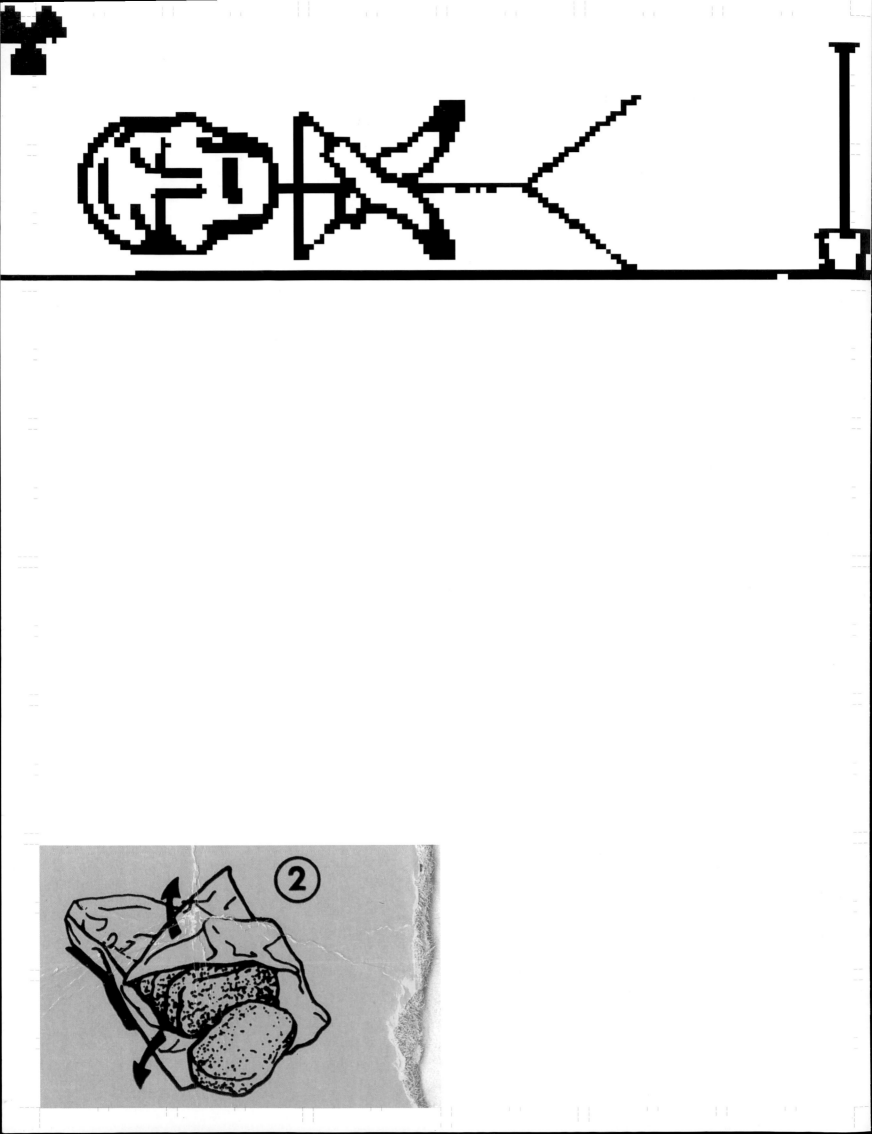

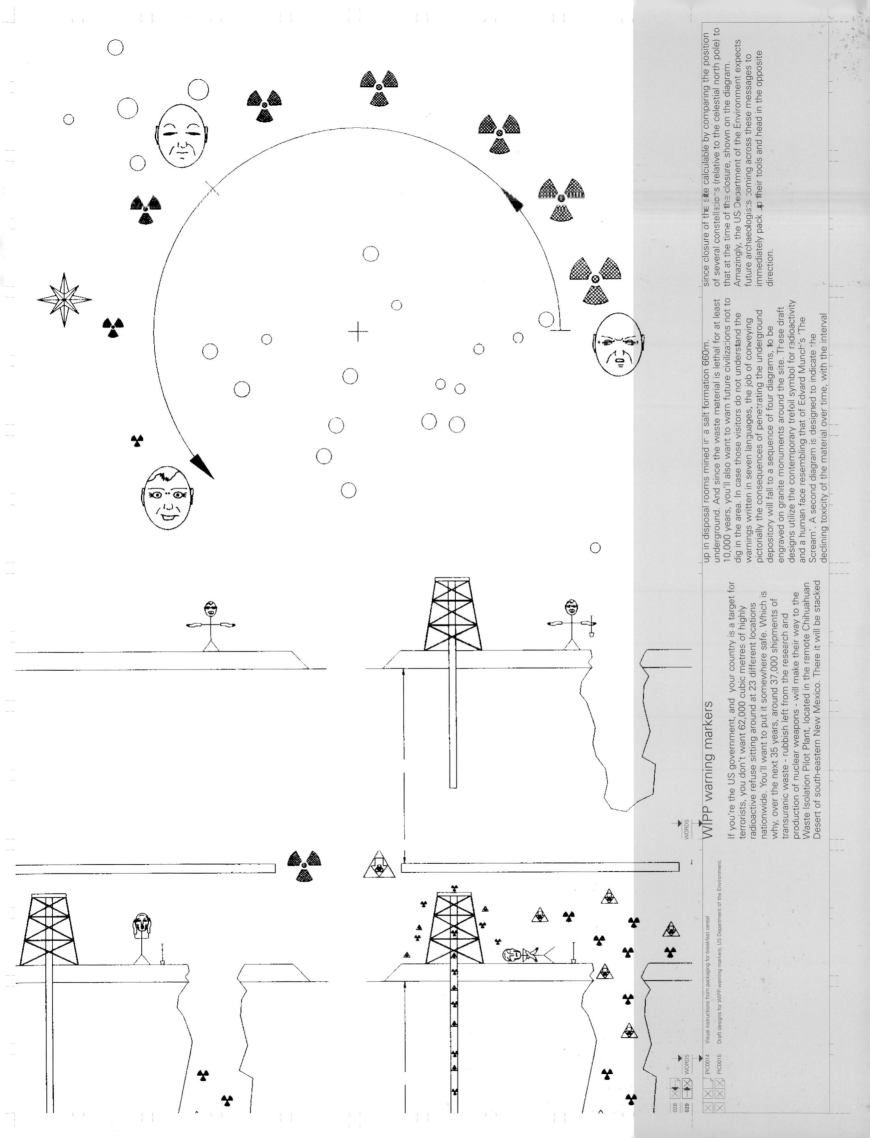

WIPP warning markers

If you're the US government, and your country is a target for terrorists, you don't want 62,000 cubic metres of highly radioactive refuse sitting around at 23 different locations nationwide. You'll want to put it somewhere safe. Which is why, over the next 35 years, around 37,000 shipments of transuranic waste - rubbish left from the research and production of nuclear weapons - will make their way to the Waste Isolation Pilot Plant, located in the remote Chihuahuan Desert of south-eastern New Mexico. There it will be stacked up in disposal rooms mined in a salt formation 660m. underground. And since the waste material is lethal for at least 10,000 years, you'll also want to warn future civilizations not to dig in the area. In case those visitors do not understand the warnings written in seven languages, the job of conveying pictorially the consequences of penetrating the underground depository will fall to a sequence of four diagrams, to be engraved on granite monuments around the site. These draft designs utilize the contemporary trefoil symbol for radioactivity and a human face resembling that of Edvard Munch's 'The Scream'. A second diagram is designed to indicate the declining toxicity of the material over time, with the interval since closure of the site calculable by comparing the position of several constellations (relative to the celestial north pole) to that at the time of the closure, shown on the diagram. Amazingly, the US Department of the Environment expects future archaeologists coming across these messages to immediately pack up their tools and head in the opposite direction.

WORDS

030
031

PICO016   Train carriage, Oslo, Norway
PICO017   Standard car dashboard display symbols

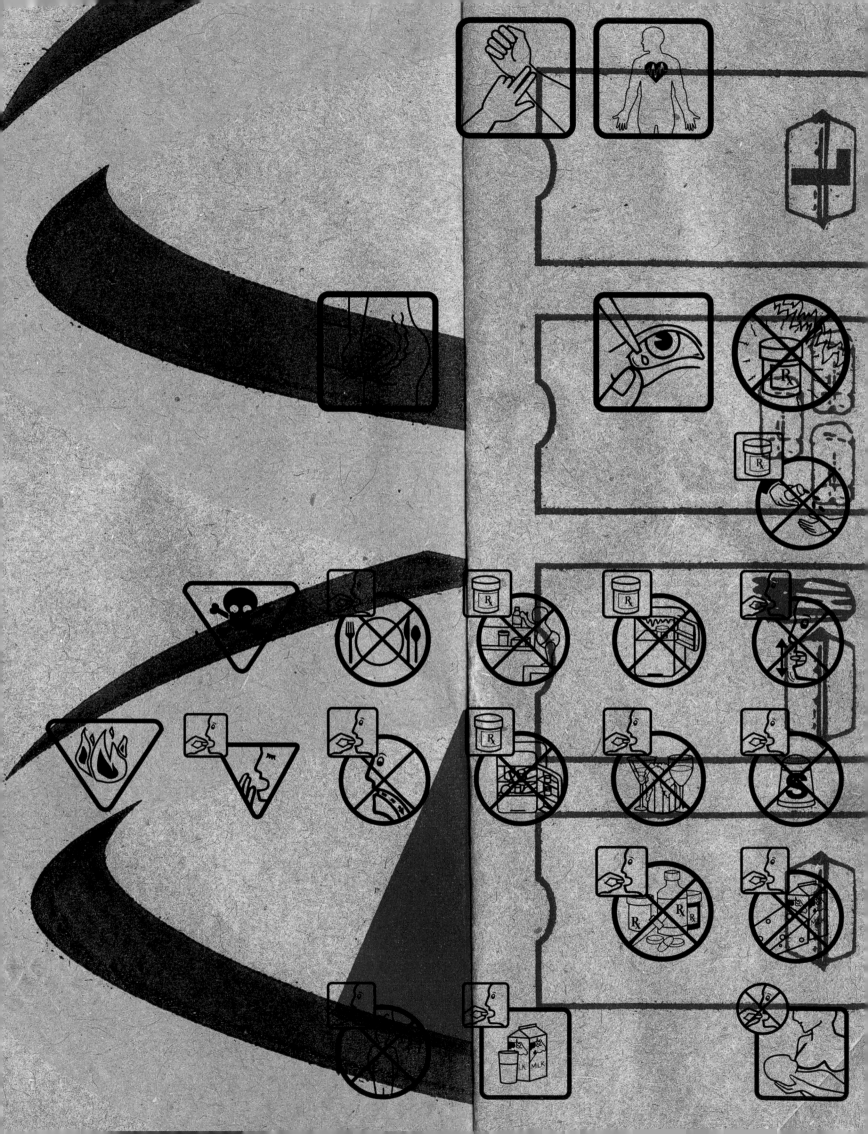

and cover a multitude of medication scenarios. Some, however, may require explanation.

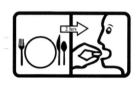
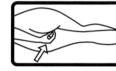
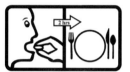

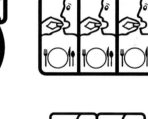

Drug packaging

Pharmaceutical companies have been deaf to calls to make advice about their products plainer and more visible on packaging. Low literacy has been proven to affect health, one recent study at the Medical College of Wisconsin concluding that HIV+ patients with low reading ability have far more difficulty adhering to medication guidelines, with an increased risk of serious immune damage. These pictograms issued by the US Pharmacopeia may be a start towards overcoming this problem. They are freely available for drug companies to use

→ WORDS
→ WORDS

PIC0018 McDonald's burger packaging
PIC0019 Drug packaging pictorial instructions and warnings © 1997 USPC

032
033

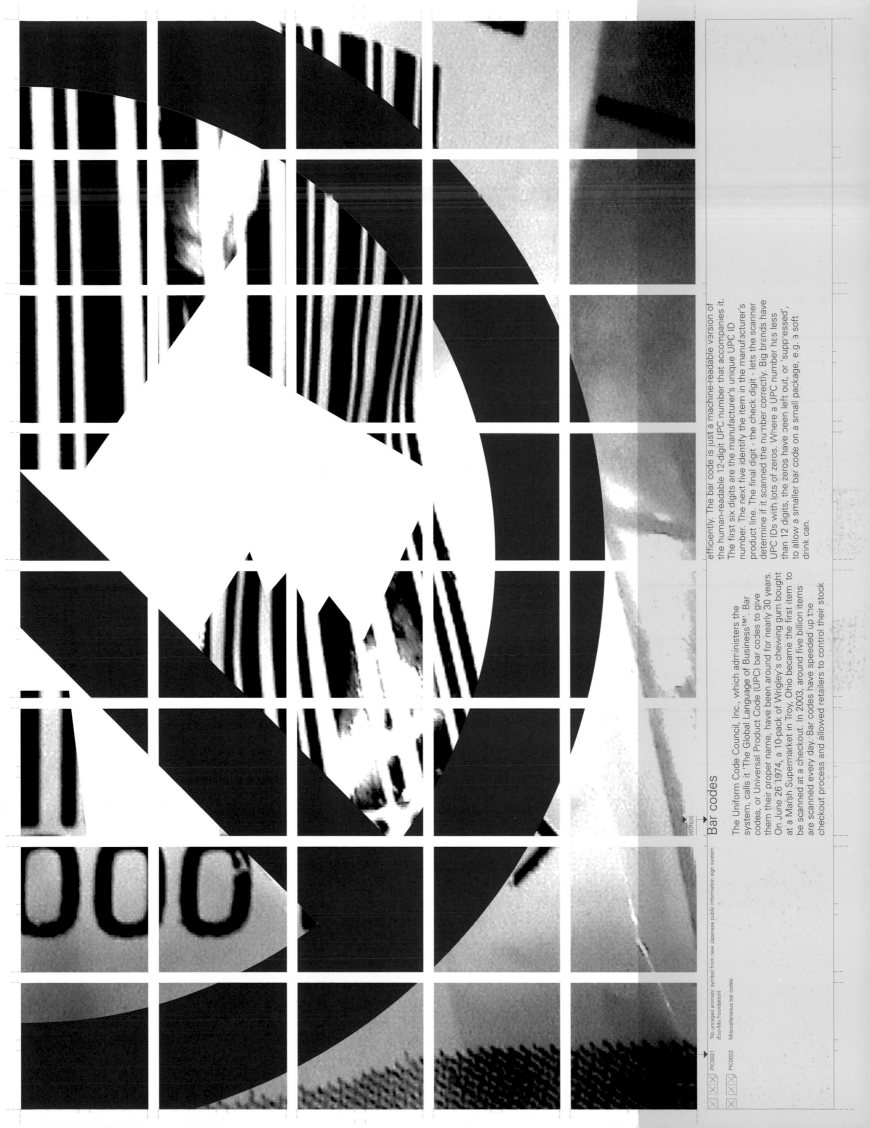

Bar codes

The Uniform Code Council, Inc., which administers the system, calls it 'The Global Language of Business™'. Bar codes, or Universal Product Code (UPC) bar codes to give them their proper name, have been around for nearly 30 years. On June 26 1974, a 10-pack of Wrigley's chewing gum bought at a Marsh Supermarket in Troy, Ohio became the first item to be scanned at a checkout. In 2003, around five billion items are scanned every day. Bar codes have speeded up the checkout process and allowed retailers to control their stock efficiently. The bar code is just a machine-readable version of the human-readable 12-digit UPC number that accompanies it. The first six digits are the manufacturer's unique UPC ID number. The next five digits are the manufacturer's product line. The final digit - the check digit - lets the scanner determine if it scanned the number correctly. Big brands have UPC IDs with lots of zeros. Where a UPC number has less than 12 digits, the zeros have been left out, or 'suppressed', to allow a smaller bar code on a small package, e.g. a soft drink can.

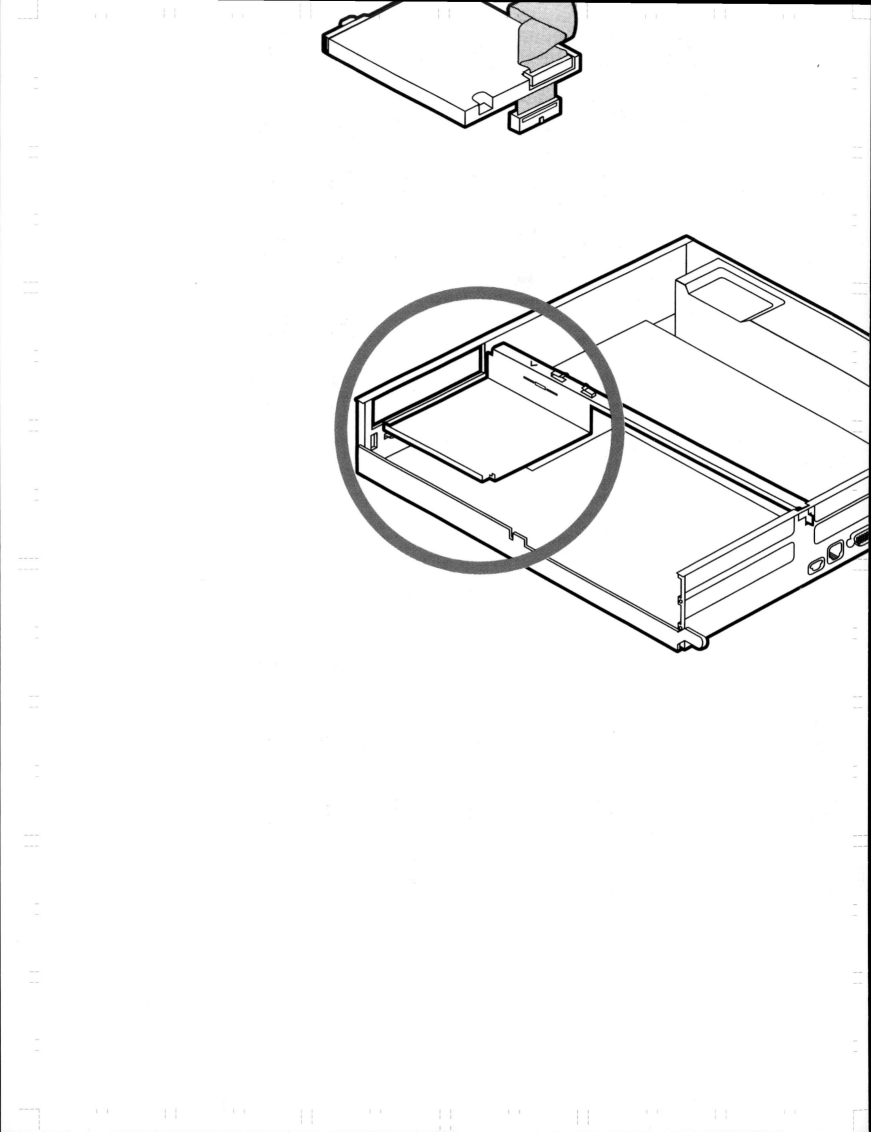

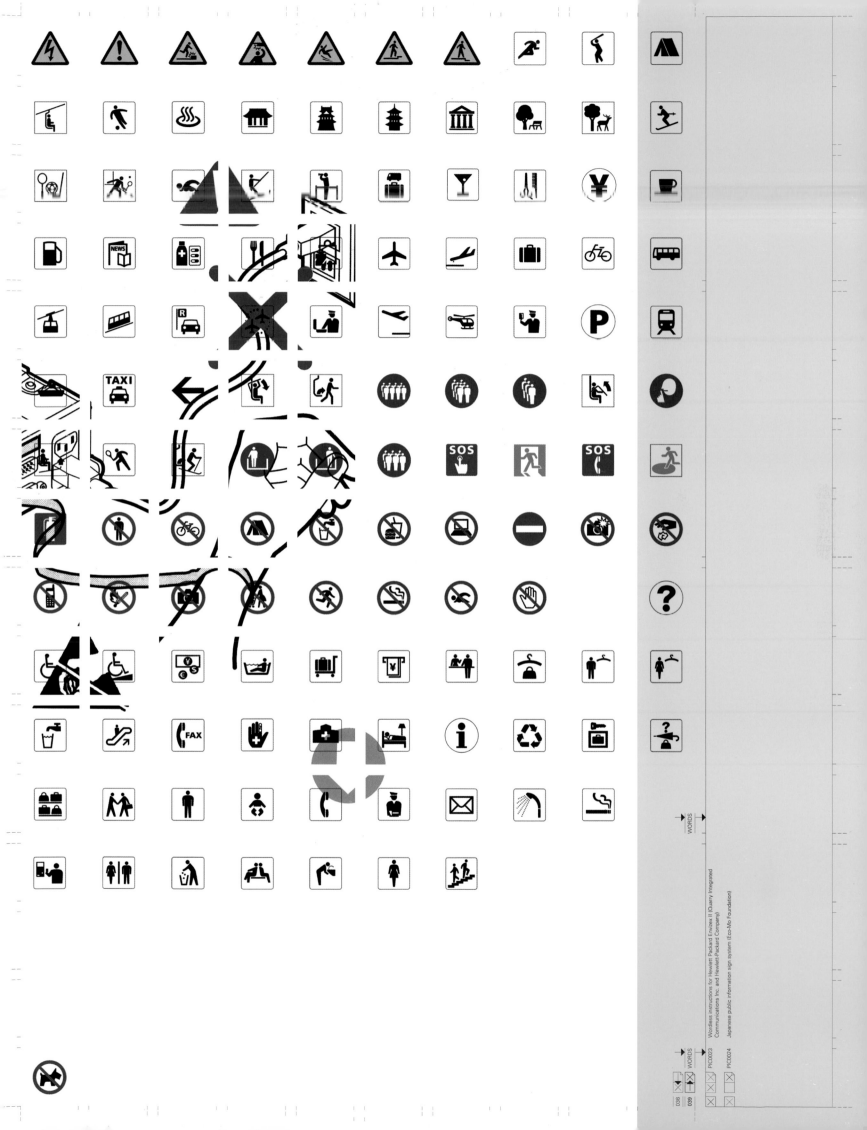

Wordless instructions for Hewlett Packard Envizex II (Quarry Integrated Communications Inc. and Hewlett-Packard Company)

Japanese public information sign system (Eco-Mo Foundation)

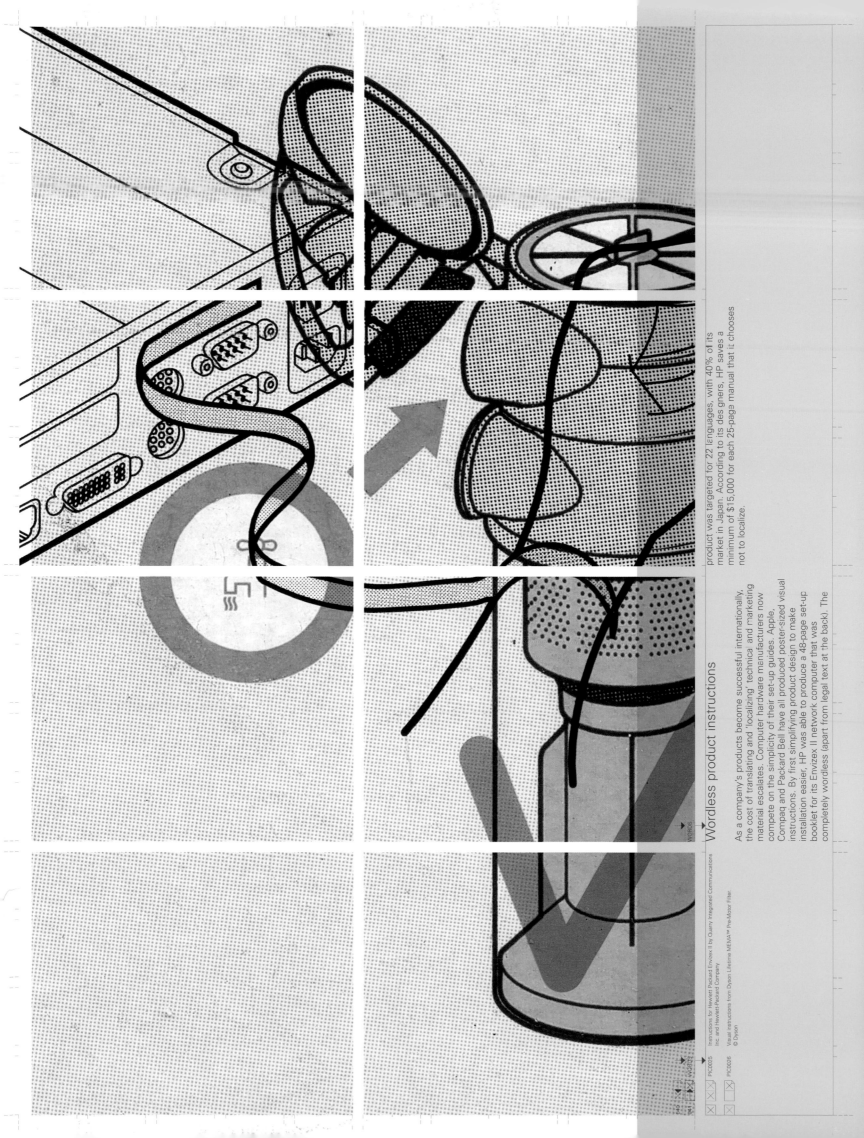

Wordless product instructions

As a company's products become successful internationally, the cost of translating and 'localizing' technical and marketing material escalates. Computer hardware manufacturers now compete on the simplicity of their set-up guides. Apple, Compaq and Packard Bell have all produced poster-sized visual instructions. By first simplifying product design to make installation easier, HP was able to produce a 48-page set-up booklet for its Envizex II network computer that was completely wordless (apart from legal text at the back). The product was targeted for 22 languages, with 40% of its market in Japan. According to its designers, HP saves a minimum of $15,000 for each 25-page manual that it chooses not to localize.

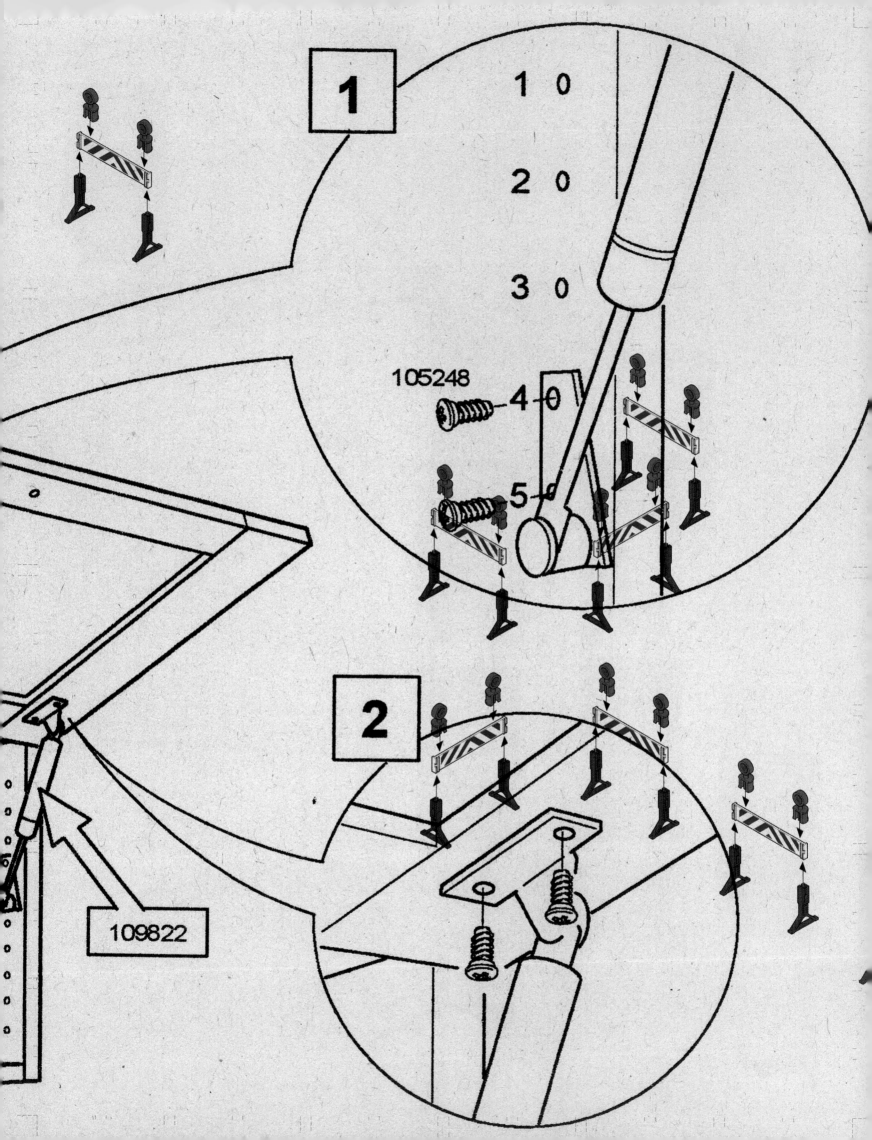

1

1 0

2 0

3 0

105248

4 0

5 0

2

109822

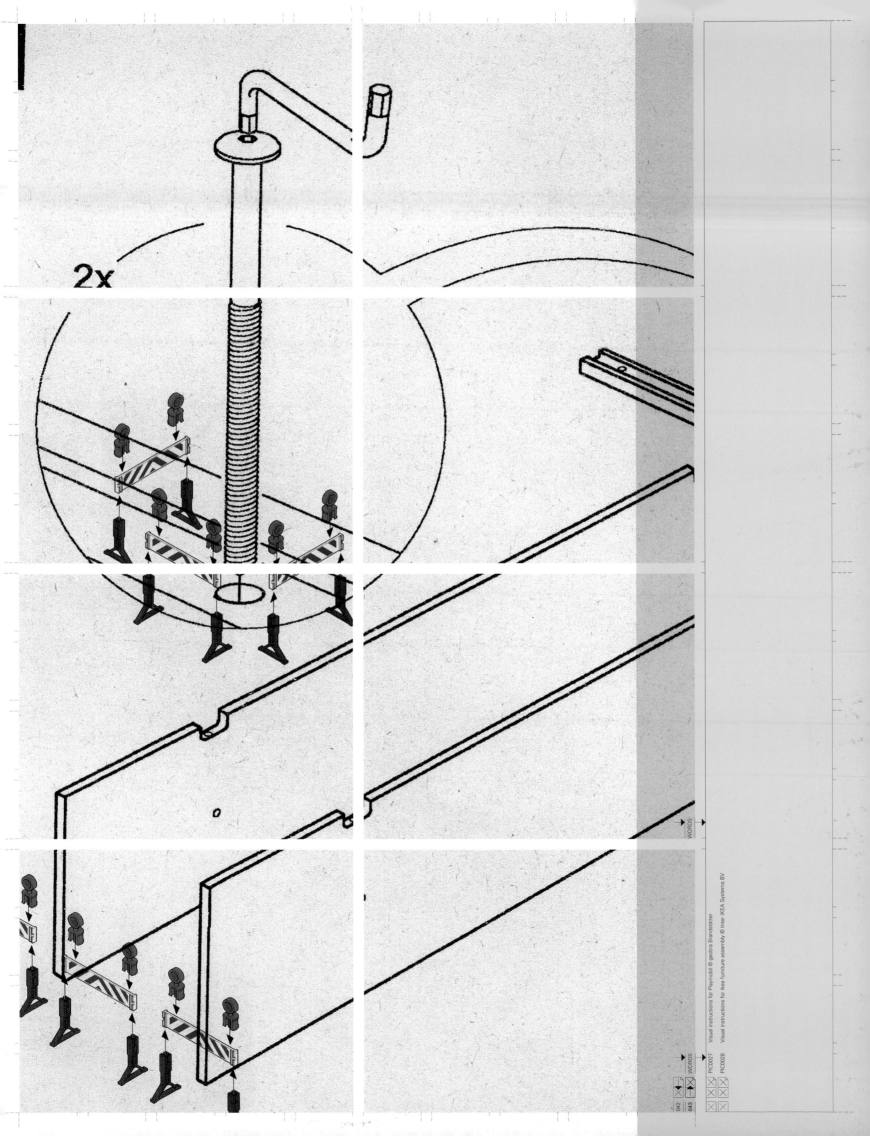

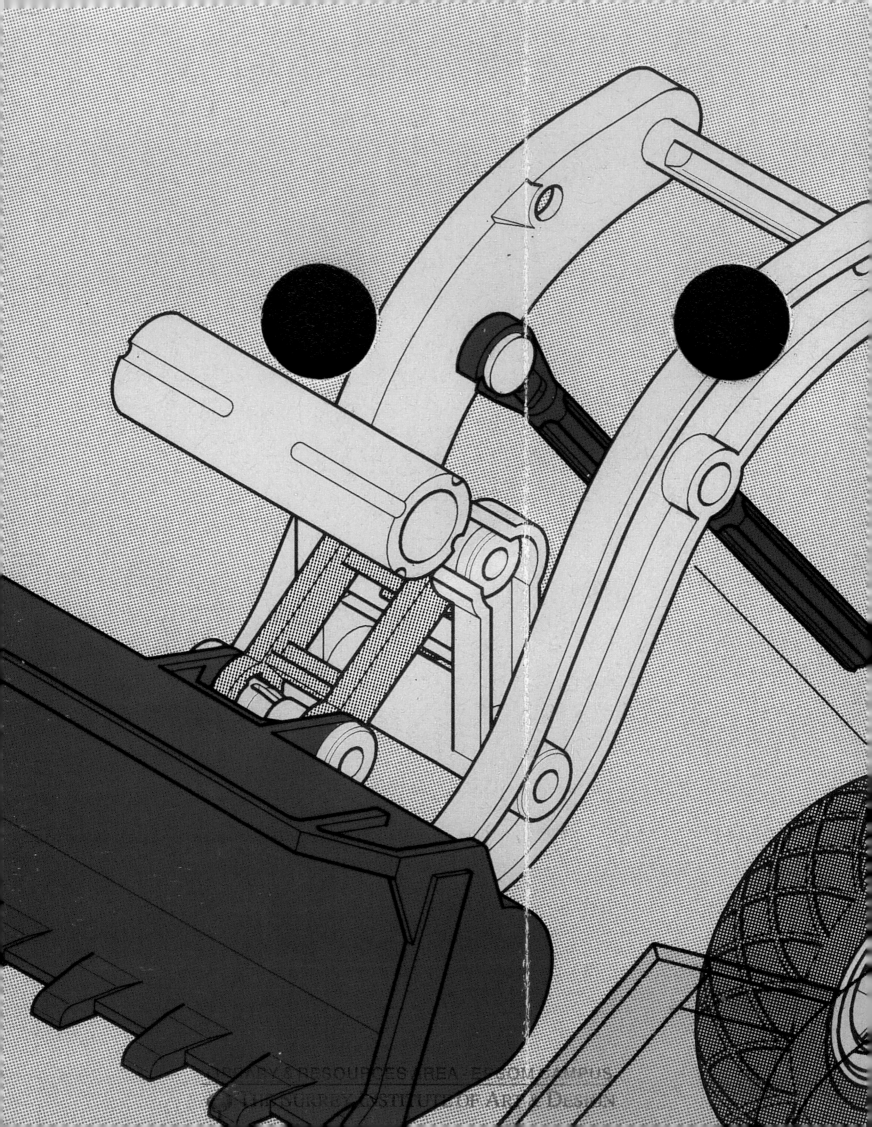

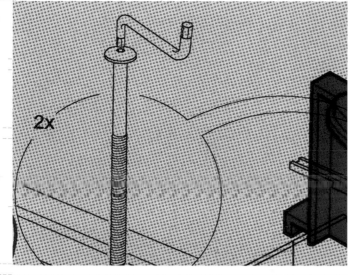

2x

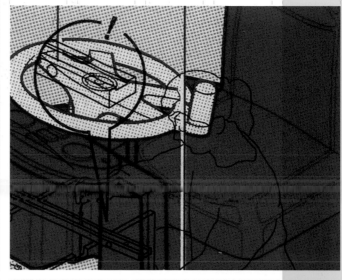

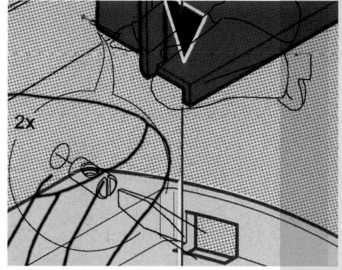

2x

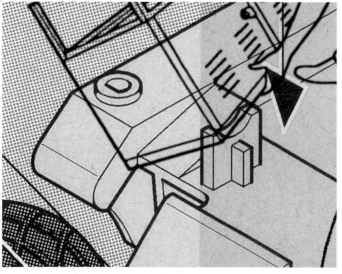

1

1   0

2   0

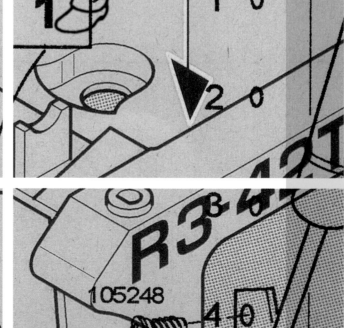

R3³ 42 1

105248

4   0

5   0

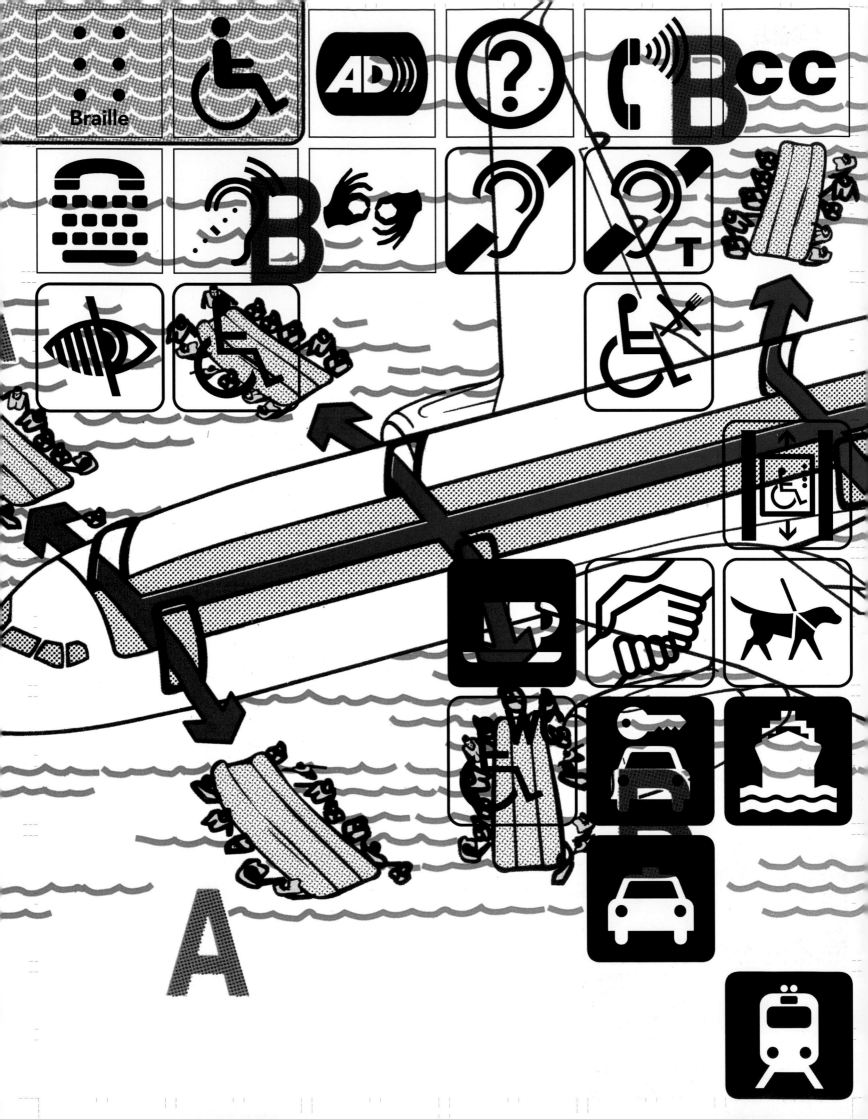

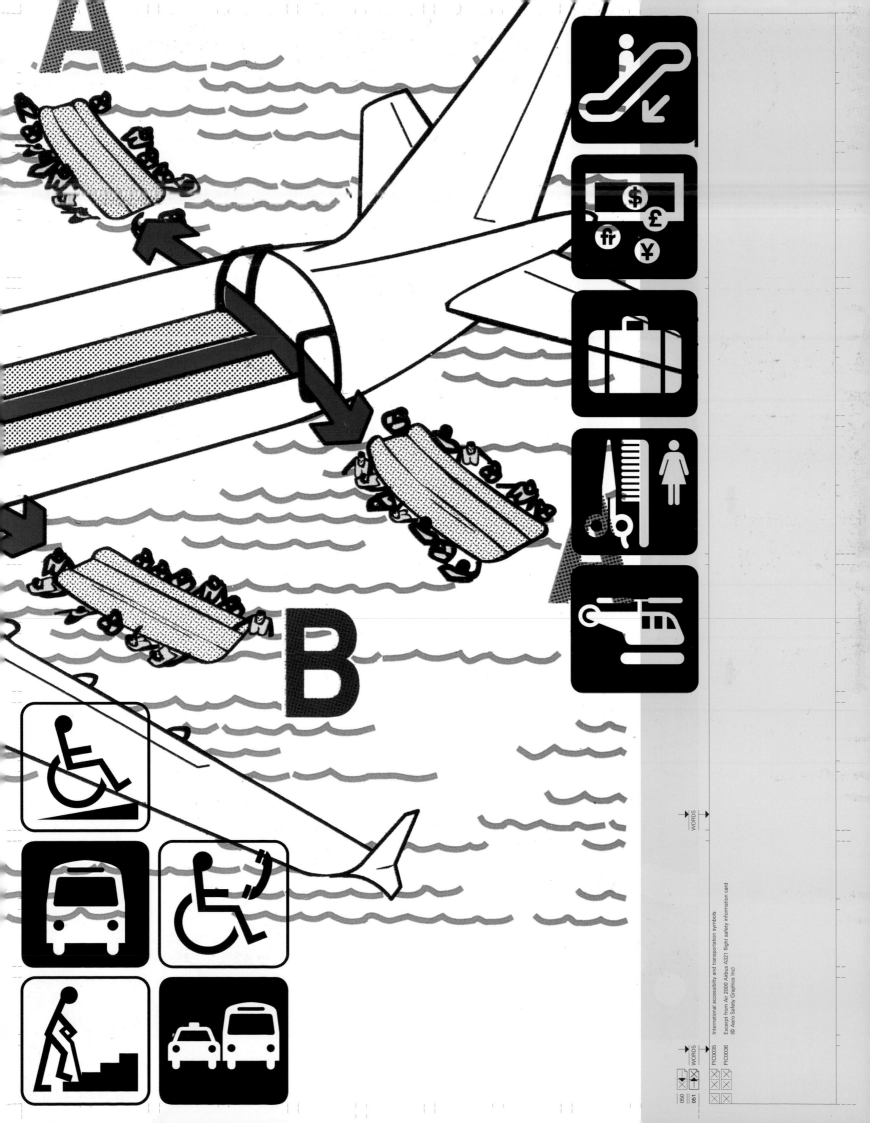

International accessibility and transportation symbols

Excerpt from Air 2000 Airbus A321 flight safety information card
(© Aero Safety Graphics Inc)

0 15400

0 325420

.4 3800

< 502

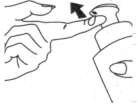

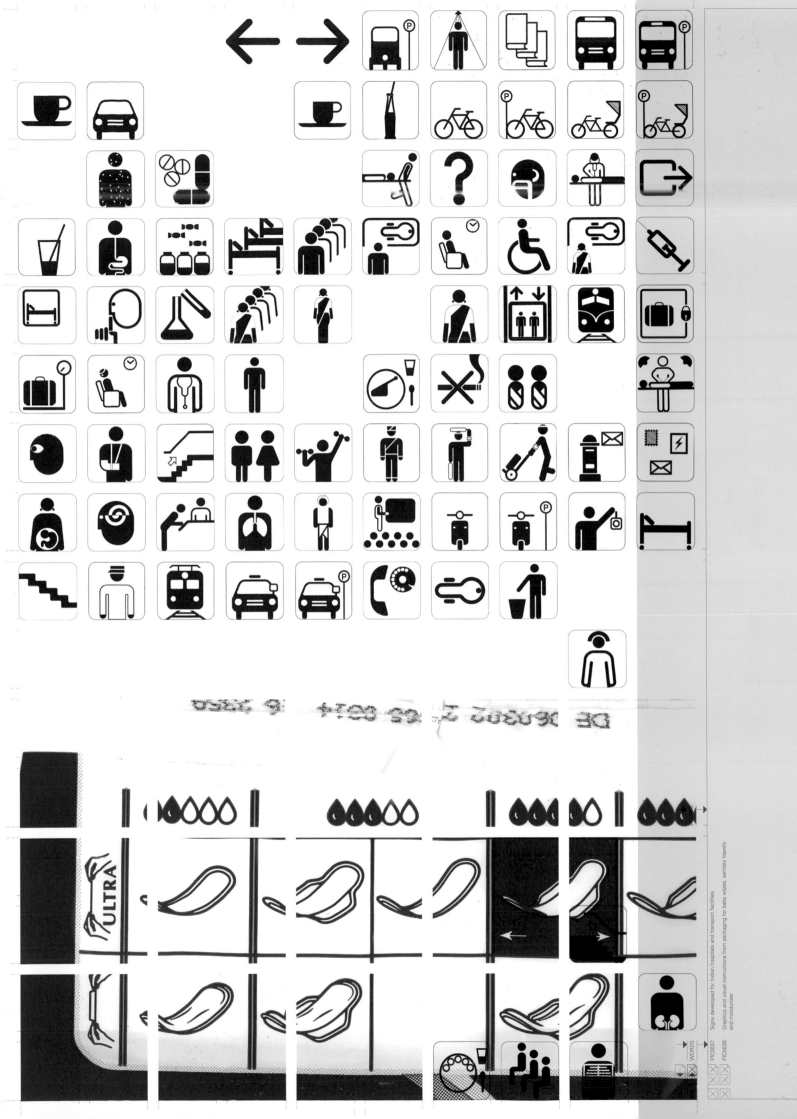

PIC0037 Signs developed for Indian hospitals and transport facilities

PIC0038 Graphics and visual instructions from packaging for baby wipes, sanitary towels and moisturiser

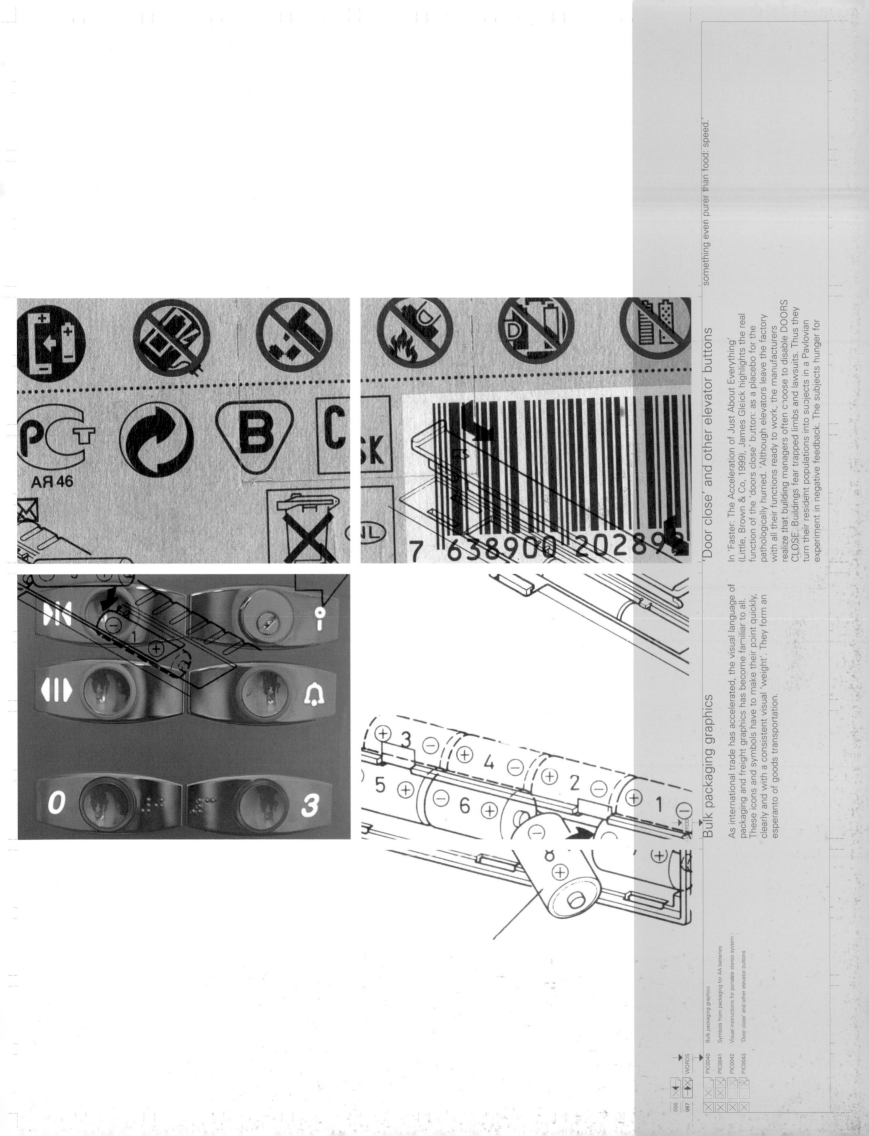

'Door close' and other elevator buttons

In 'Faster: The Acceleration of Just About Everything' (Little, Brown & Co, 1999), James Gleick highlights the real function of the 'doors close' button: as a placebo for the pathologically hurried. 'Although elevators leave the factory with all their functions ready to work, the manufacturers realize that building managers often choose to disable DOORS CLOSE. Buildings fear trapped limbs and lawsuits. Thus they turn their resident populations into subjects in a Pavlovian experiment in negative feedback. The subjects hunger for

Bulk packaging graphics

As international trade has accelerated, the visual language of packaging and freight graphics has become familiar to all. These icons and symbols have to make their point quickly, clearly and with a consistent visual 'weight'. They form an esperanto of goods transportation.

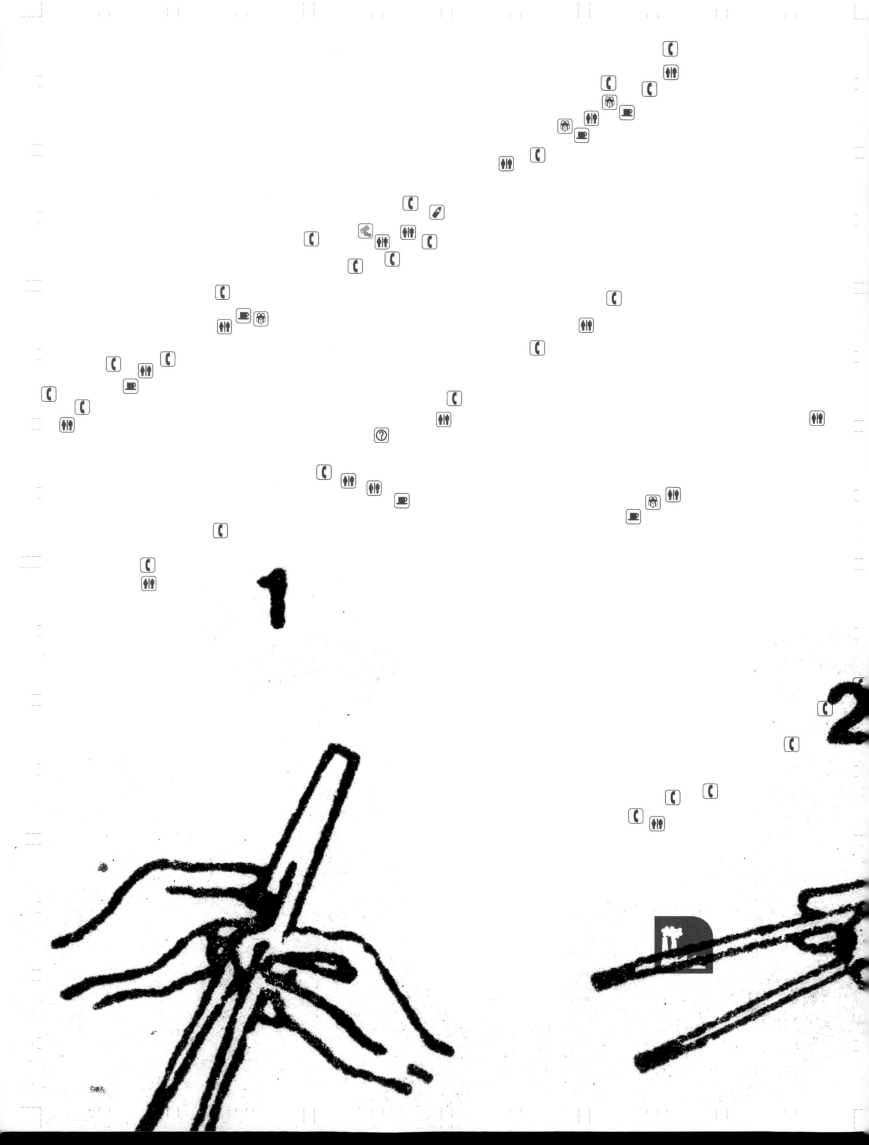

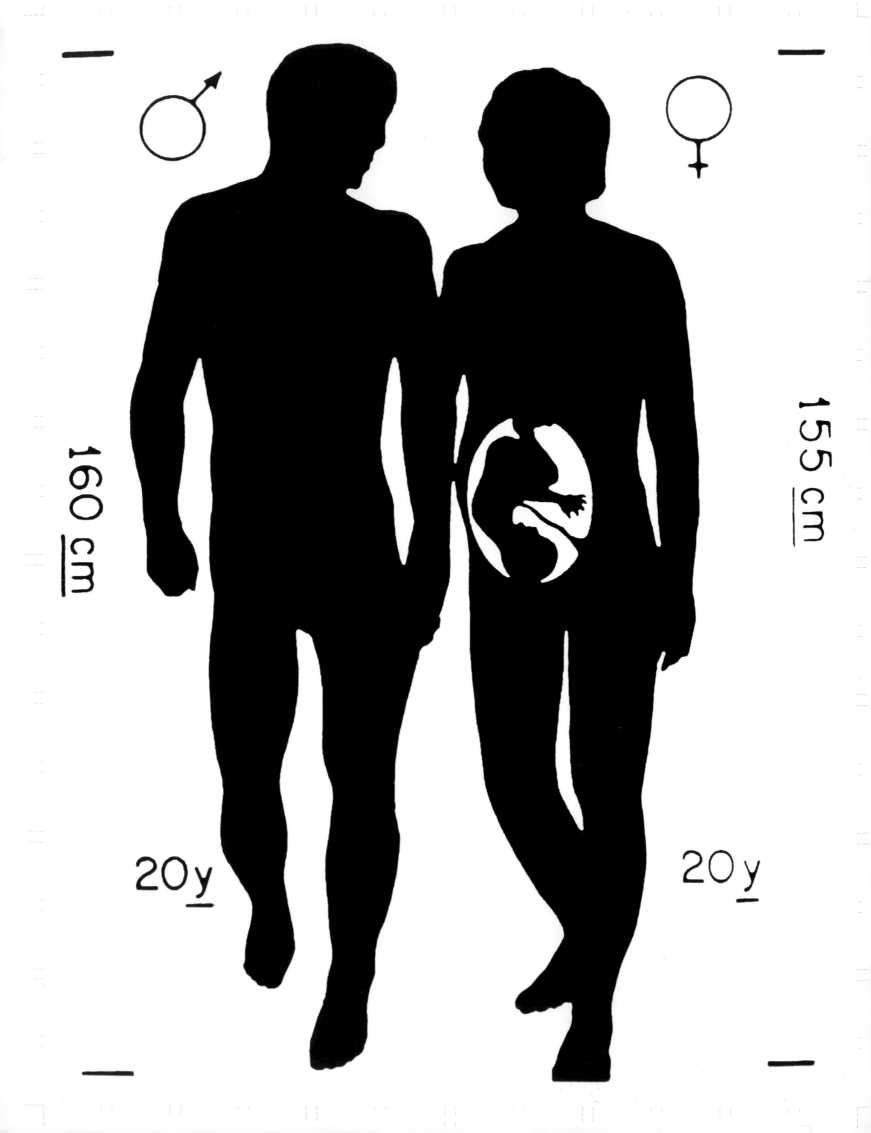

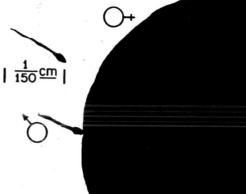

| 120 cm |

120 cm

| $\frac{1}{150}$ cm |

WORDS

Voyager space probe diagrams

Designing for universal understanding is one thing. Conceiving graphic information to be understood by creatures from another galaxy is another. NASA's Voyager One and Two space probes escaped the solar system back in 1990 and are still hurtling through the void, but they are unlikely to approach another planetary system for at least 40,000 years. The 'Golden Record' placed on board the twin probes in 1977 was intended to communicate the story of earth to extraterrestrials. Compiled by a committee chaired by Carl Sagan, the 12-inch gold-plated copper phonograph disc contained images and sounds, and was encased in an aluminium jacket with a cartridge, needle and symbolic instructions on how it should be played. It included a series of silhouetted images by Jon Lomberg that attempted to relate the most fundamental features of human existence - reproduction, predation etc. - to any alien intelligence that might discover them. Each silhouette relates to the next image on the record, its colour photograph. An alien would have to discern for itself the meaning of '160cm', '20y', gender symbols and the concept of male and female.

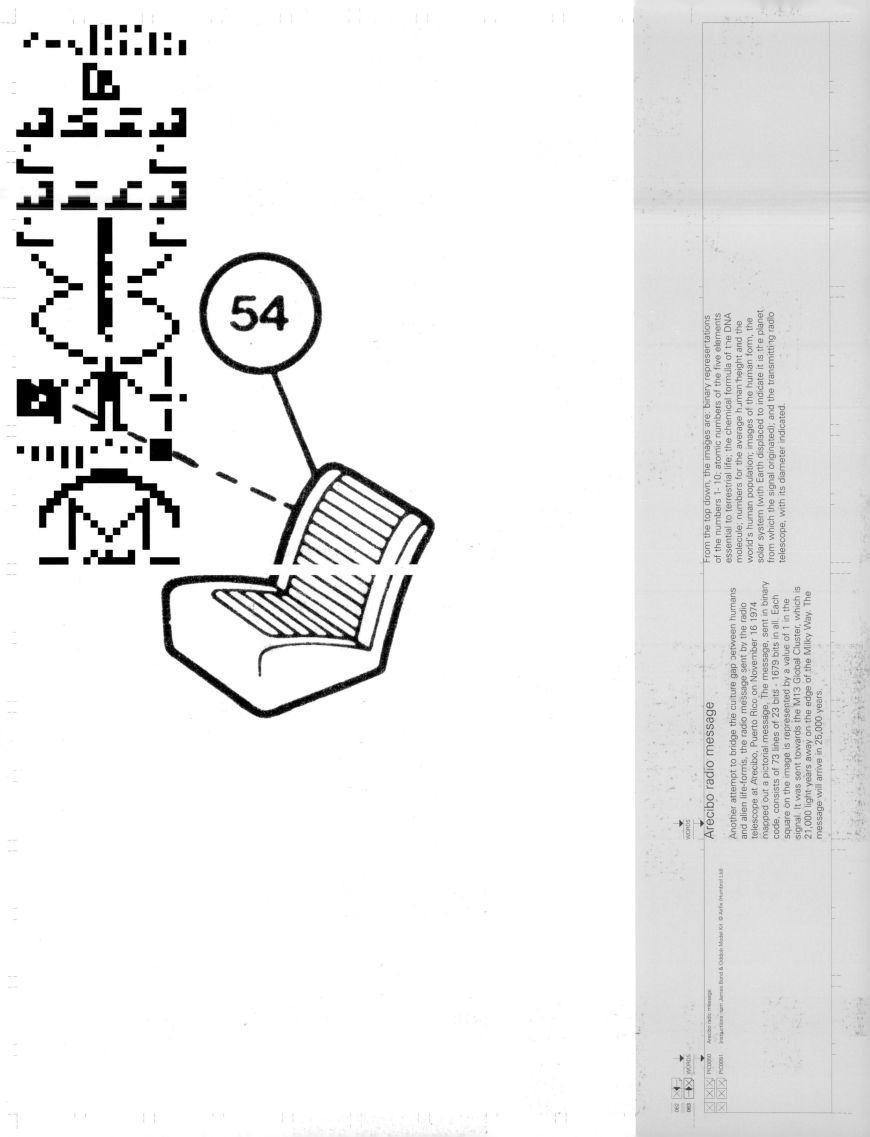

Arecibo radio message

Another attempt to bridge the culture gap between humans and alien life-forms, the radio message sent by the radio telescope at Arecibo, Puerto Rico on November 16 1974 mapped out a pictorial message. The message, sent in binary code, consists of 73 lines of 23 bits - 1679 bits in all. Each square on the image is represented by a value of 1 in the signal. It was sent towards the M13 Global Cluster, which is 21,000 light years away on the edge of the Milky Way. The message will arrive in 25,000 years.

From the top down, the images are: binary representations of the numbers 1-10; atomic numbers of the five elements essential to terrestrial life; the chemical formula of the DNA molecule; numbers for the average human height and the world's human population; images of the human form, the solar system (with Earth displaced to indicate it is the planet from which the signal originated); and the transmitting radio telescope, with its diameter indicated.

f/22	**f/16**	**f/11**

Visual instructions from packaging for camera film

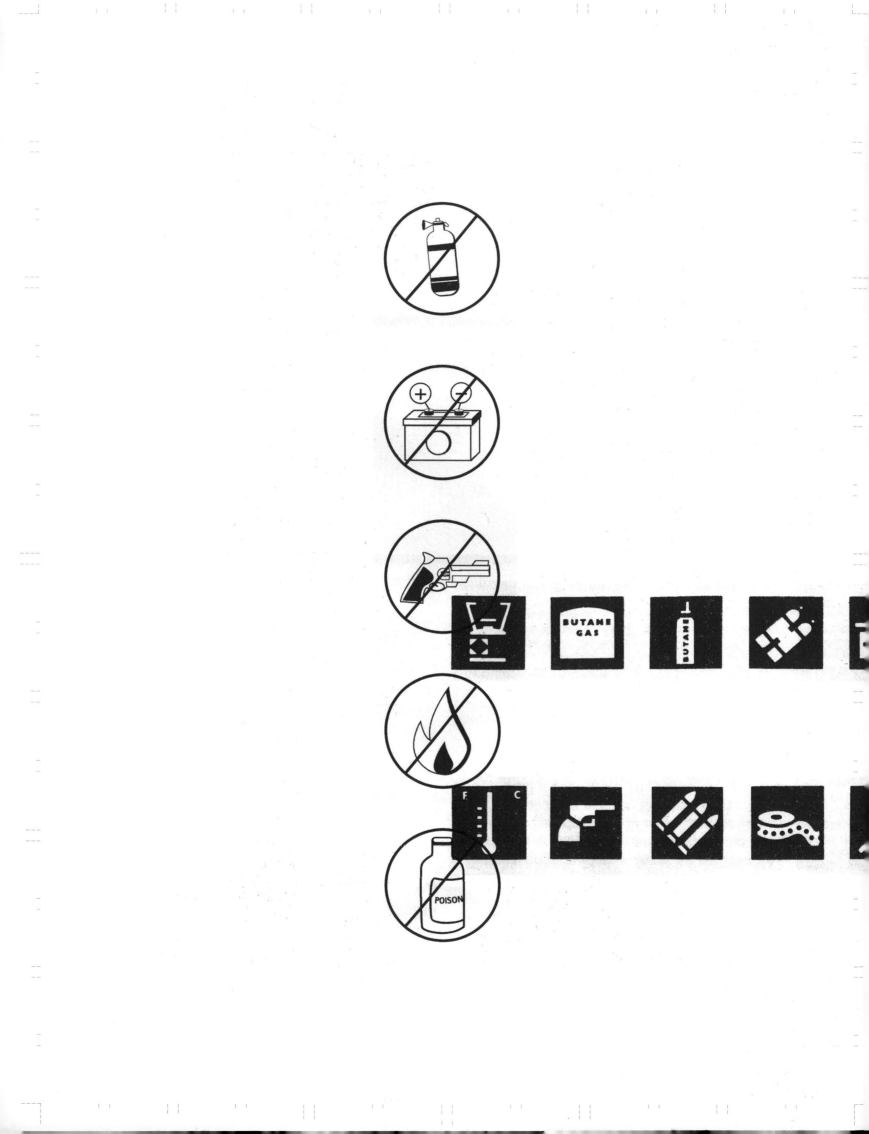

WORDS

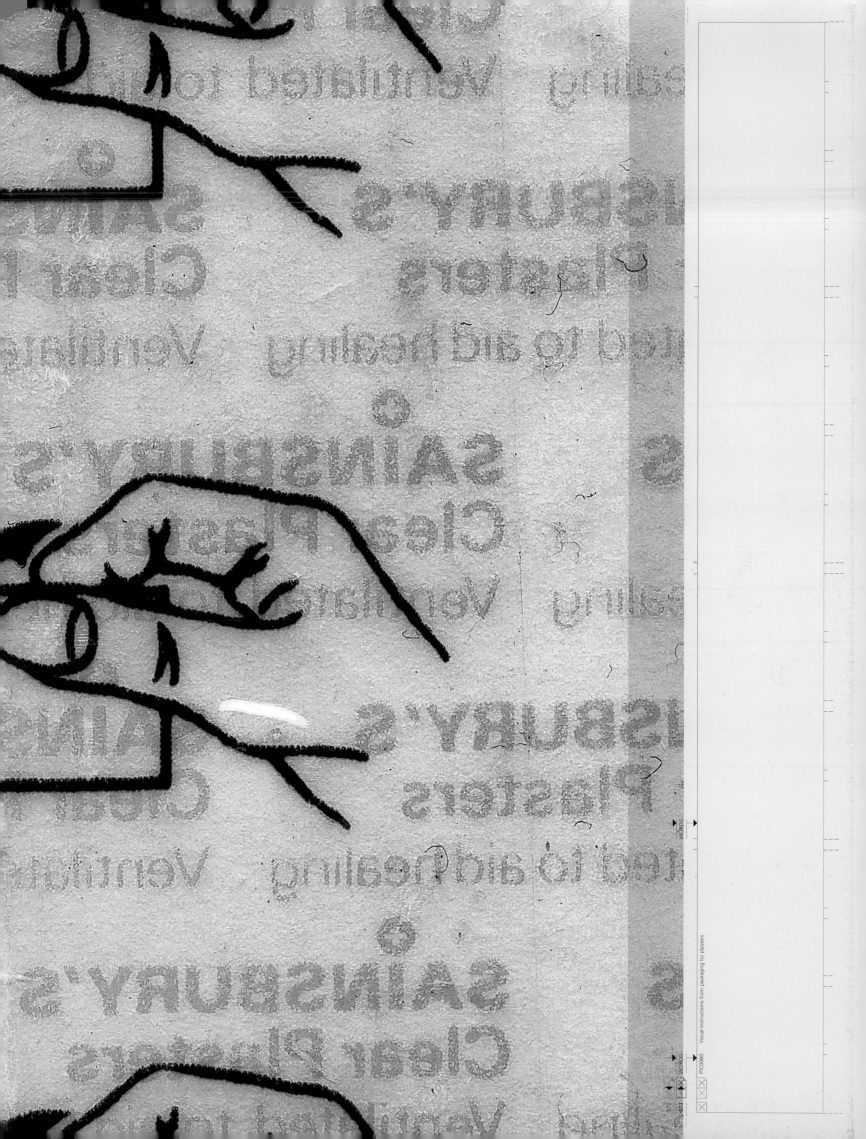

Voices in the crowd

Universalized signs and symbols drape a film of visual shorthand across our everyday experience. They govern our behaviour towards public places and amenities, traffic systems, packaged consumer goods, household appliances, electronics, motor vehicles and the Internet. We scarcely even register this web of figures, shapes, outlines and silhouettes, let alone its influence on our actions. And why should we? The whole point of this stuff – and the reason why we never question it – is that it is reproduced with mind-numbing consistency. It's the same everywhere you go, isn't it?

Not so. Thankfully, very little is uniform from country to country. It's a complete misconception to believe that, by removing words from the equation, graphic information becomes magically accessible to everyone, everywhere. Visual shorthand is a social construct. Our interpretation of icons and symbols depends heavily on what cultural baggage we unpack in the process. So it's not surprising to find that the sign systems that Western citizens take for granted at airports, railway stations and hospitals are being amended in non-Western countries to make more sense to local populations.

In fact, the real diversity of wordless graphic communication is to be found not in international symbols and global branding programmes but in applications developed at the regional, local and personal levels. There are those that aim to overcome language differences or illiteracy among large audiences: airlines' passenger safety instructions, city subway maps, low-literacy healthcare information, local sign systems, and so on. And there are those that have arisen out of the need for individuals to communicate, one-to-one, amongst themselves, and which take the form of visual codes. It is here, in our attempts to convey information and emotion to each other, via channels as new as the Internet but as insensitive to human expression as stone, that the frontiers of graphic communication are being rolled back.

All the same, but different

Bringing a frontierless world one step closer was the aim of the protocol passed by the UN World Conference on Road and Motor Transport in Geneva in 1949, which harmonized road signs from country to country. It set in stone (or sheet metal) for all eternity the silhouetted figures that would oversee half the world's driving behaviour. However, like armies of identical cartoon emigrants sent forth from culturally neutral Switzerland, these figures have had over half a century to absorb the cultural characteristics of their adopted homelands.

The 'men at work' warning sign is a case in point. Across Europe today, one can find as many departures from this particular norm as there were signatories to the original red-triangle standard. Belgian and Danish signs feature a workman equipped with a helmet,

useless broken glass and tipped the lot into the harbour.

Local audiences have to be addressed in visual languages that they are familiar with. It's a fact that international standards organizations and global businesses are having to face. In the realm of public information signs, where there has been the most energy expended by standards agencies in trying to enforce a global standard, there is increasing divergence between countries and cultures. Standard signs are not just being redrawn in new styles; new signs are being developed that reflect local needs and thereby help to generate local sign dialects.

Standard deviations

In India, for example, a system of symbol-based signs for use in hospitals answers a long-felt need in the country, which is home to 14 major languages and 1600 dialects. The absence of a familiar, non-verbal system for guiding patients, visitors and staff was leading to chaos. Professor Ravi Poovaiah of the Indian Institute of Technology's Industrial Design Centre, who designed the new system, claims that 35–40 per cent of first-time users of Bombay hospitals ended up standing in the wrong queue. Using ideas for visual representations of hospital departments generated by themselves and a sample group of users, Poovaiah's team created a set of solutions that were then redrawn, made graphically compatible, and are now in use in Indian hospitals. Taking the standard Isotype man as its starting point, the set includes 21 symbols for hospital departments, from pediatrics to urology, that, for the most part, are distinct and easily understood. They would be welcomed by hospital users anywhere.

But the Indian signs also include a number of variants on the kind of standard signs found at public facilities all over the world. By more accurately reflecting their cultural context, these variations eliminate the distracting cultural faux pas of would-be universal sign systems. The woman in the sign for female toilet, for example, wears a sari not a Western mini-dress. Divisions of wealth, class and gender in India have necessitated an additional sign for 'rural man' – in addition to signs for 'man' and 'woman' – which shows Isotype man in a white turban and traditional Hindu dress. And since one does not even a new sign system can do much about waiting times, there are symbols for 'male queue' and 'female queue'. These uniquely Indian symbols are shared by an accompanying sign system for railway interchanges, which has its own cultural idiosyncracies. As well as symbols for 'cycle-rickshaw parking' and 'cigarette stall', there are signs for 'men's waiting room' and 'ladies' waiting room'. Many of these signs obviously reinforce discriminatory attitudes prevalent in Indian society. All that any successful sign system does is passively reflect prevailing cultural norms. However, the Indian system is an outstanding example of how a Western-based, standardized, 'international' sign set can be actively improved upon by local designers.

same time offering a symbolic link to life above ground.

Subway graphics, public information signs, aircraft safety instructions – they all communicate, subliminally, that you, the citizen-consumer, are part of a system, and are expected to obey the rules. They are formal, impersonal, unequivocal, expressionless. However, not all information is so coldly insistent. Sometimes it has to be able to reason, to persuade, to make a personal appeal, or to express human emotion. On these occasions, words can just get in the way.

Arts of persuasion

Pictures with human detail, rendered in a fashion familiar to the audience, can have infinitely more impact than a set of bullet points, especially when advice is being dispensed. Aircraft safety instructions go some of the way. In many developing countries, healthcare information pamphlets in the form of cartoon-style narratives go further. These commonly carry no text at all, and are intended to be understood by a large population of non-readers. Typically, the cautionary tale is depicted of a man/woman/couple/family who follow/don't follow the advice they have received. A pamphlet from El Salvador on female sterilization ('La Operacion') begins with a couple being plagued by three pesky infants. Pretty soon (by the very next panel), they are discussing sterilization (symbolized by a shared speech bubble with a simple diagram of some tied-up fallopian tubes), while stripping cobs of corn. Following the swift, painless procedure (denoted by a clock on the wall and the woman's cheery smile upon waking from anaesthetic), the husband is soon holding forth to his compadres about the wonders of the female non-reproductive system. Needless to say, even the kids are better behaved by the end.

Patronizing though it may sometimes seem, visual storytelling of this kind can help to soften hard issues and overcome fears or apprehension among the audience. Human figures showing human emotions make much better models than stick figures or icons. Cultural and ethnic cues (clothing, settings, skin colour, etc.) help still further. It's a technique that hasn't been lost on other, less charitable interests. In the Gulf War in 1991, the US Army's Psychological Operations (Psyops) Division went into overdrive, leafleting Iraqi troops with a variety of visual propaganda, most of it outstandingly crudely drawn and designed either to sow doubts among enemy ranks about their commanders or demoralize them.

To try to engender trust and a sense of Arab brotherhood, beards were added to allied soldiers. Schoolboy-standard sketches encouraged Iraqi soldiers to think of their families and surrender rather than face a terrifying onslaught. Usually, such a warning would be followed up within 24 hours by bombs, to establish credibility. An astonishing 44 per cent of Iraqi troops deserted. The most professional example depicted the force of US Marines as a knife-wielding, wailing tidal

Some Turkish and Spanish workers have billowing, rolled-up sleeves. Their British colleague wears wellingtons. And the standard Frenchman's head seems unnaturally big, given the size of his frame. Even within most of these countries, variable workmanship means there is no absolute uniformity or conformity. (For more on cultural variations of standard road signs, see Bartolomeo Mecanico's Traffic Signs of the World at www.elve.net/rcoulst.htm)

These may be inconsequential differences, as far as driving goes. After all, in each of these countries, the workman appears as a black silhouette on a white background within a red equilateral triangle. There is no doubt as to the meaning. Yet these small oscillations from one of the most established international sign standards do indicate an underlying resistance to the principle of cultural neutrality. In many cases, they reveal entertaining glimpses of a state's self-image and preoccupations. They expose the folly of prescribing, to too precise a formula, the means of expression that a society employs within its own boundaries. How would we react if the language we used in conversation was suddenly subject to the rules and restrictions of a universal house style?

God is in the details. Verbal communication is infinitely diverse. The way a language such as English is spoken varies from country to country, region to region, person to person, and yet meaning is rarely lost, despite differences in accent or dialect. Once a language is established it is free to evolve and become an expression of different cultural identities. So it should be with visual communication. The example of the men at work road sign reveals just how much extra cultural information can be smuggled through in ostensibly neutral material. But it also brings to light how individual societies modify so-called universal visual languages – consciously or unconsciously – for their own cultural purposes

Needless to say, when a visual language is foreign to its readers, misinterpretations occur. In many African states, high illiteracy rates compel local manufacturers to design packaging that features illustrations of exactly what is inside. It's a visual language that African citizen-consumers are used to. Hardly surprising, then, that when Gerber started selling baby food in Africa, packaged US-style with a beautiful Caucasian baby on the label, there wasn't a huge amount of interest. Or that when a cargo of boxes stamped with the international symbol for 'fragile' – a wine glass with a snapped stem – arrived in one African port, stevedores took it for a consignment of

Even in cases where a universal solution to a design problem could be adopted, international businesses often have no interest in co-operating, usually because they are rivals. For example, you would have thought that, by now, there might be a single, harmonized design for passenger aircraft evacuation instructions. By and large, the messages they convey about what to do, where to go and how to save yourself are similar, and the way they are conveyed – via wordless, illustrated, laminated cards – is the same. No one speaks: the imperilled passengers leave the plane in orderly fashion, some even wearing a smile. And yet there is no consistency to the designs. Every airline produces its own card because it is in an industry where any and every difference from one's competitors is worth preserving. And since nationality or some form of cultural identity plays a large role in the brand image of most airlines, that too has to be reflected in all of their graphic outputs. Even though, at the level of information design, some of the instructions are indescribably poor, the graphic diversity that this wilful opposition produces is staggering, and quite inspiring.

Take almost any form of visual information and you will find a wonderful lack of consistency between solutions arrived at in different cultures. All around the world there are organizations and individuals devising new ways of conveying similar information to other organizations and individuals. But they are doing it with their own specific audiences in mind. Underground railways, for example, generally follow the model of identifying individual lines by colour and individual stations by their name. However, there are two cities on opposite sides of the world that do things differently. Stations on the underground networks of Mexico City and Fukuoka, Japan are identified not just by name, but also by picture. Most stops or the nine lines of Mexico's Red del Metro are assigned their own pictogram. The variety of languages and dialects among the city's vast working population, and the high level of illiteracy, means that some form of non-verbal signposting is essential. But the pictograms do more than help people get around. By symbolizing fragments of local culture – events, personalities, buildings, objects, etc. – associated with each station, they offer a little window on every district, and form a uniquely democratic urban history, with each part of the city equally represented. Not unlike the crests of the 17 contrada of Siena, the subway symbols of Mexico City compose a city-wide, neighbourhood-based heraldry. In Fukuoka, the much less complex system achieves a similar feat, ostensibly guiding foreign visitors around the subway, while at the

wave, backed up by warships and jet fighters, sending heavily moustachioed Iraqi troops fleeing for their lives. Twelve thousand copies were placed in sealed bottles and tossed into the Gulf off Kuwait, with the hope that the Iraqis would pick them up and interpret the message as a sign of an imminent landing by the Americans. Deception as well as intimidation was behind the message in these particular bottles.

Ten years later, information warfare was being waged again, in Afghanistan. This time the aim was to drive a wedge between the civilian population and the hated ruling Taleban. The 70 per cent illiteracy rate in the country demanded a campaign of visual propaganda. Most leaflets encouraged betrayal of Taleban leaders: one showed leader Mullah Mohammed Omar targeted by the cross hairs of a gun scope, while another showed disturbing scenes of Al-Qaeda terrorists and public floggings. Of more practical use to most ordinary Afghans was the leaflet showing them with the aid of a series of full-colour cartoons what to do with the yellow packets marked 'HDR', being dropped by US planes. However, pictures can be just as misleading as words: tear open one of these Humanitarian Daily Rations, the cartoon seems to say, and you have a feast for your entire family. Perhaps the associations it made, between the stars and stripes on the HDR packet and the smiling Afghan faces, were considered more important than the message's factual accuracy.

Express yourself

Of course, modern technologies and electronic media have handed us el – artists and non-artists – powerful tools for tampering with the truth. With pictures hogging the limelight, we no longer have to try and find precisely the right words. Fans of PowerPoint, Microsoft's ubiquitous text-and-graphics presentation software, claim that it gives visual, three-dimensional shape to arguments, overcoming the linear limitations of language. Critics counter that it is seen by too many people as a replacement for human contact and discussion, and as an easy way to gloss over the flaws in an argument. Either way, Microsoft estimates that around 30 million PowerPoint presentations are made every day. Executives are busying themselves by formatting slides, selecting backgrounds and embellishing their bullet points not with a few well-chosen words but with 'Screen Beans': silhouetted stick figures that signify concepts such as 'a good idea' (with a lightbulb above its head) and 'puzzlement' (with a scratch of the head). Even religion is coming through a projector today. Preachers buy PowerPoint sermons on CD-Rom and customize them with backdrops of sunrises, hellfire or scenes from the Holy Land. The website www.powerpointsermons.com describes the effect: 'One pastor reported, "Our altars were full and folks were weeping and making heartfelt decisions."'

Robert E. Horn, visiting scholar at Stanford University, predicts an increasingly sophisticated use of 'visual language' – a tightly integrated mesh of text and graphics – in everyday communication. Clip art, he argues, offers an almost inexhaustible range of images that will soon be liberally sprinkled throughout professional presentations and documents 'to get across the point in ways that text by itself never could do'.

It's a technique that Galileo was using four centuries ago when he inserted tiny line drawings of the planets into his astronomical texts. And it's one that millions of people are experimenting with every day when they compose emails. 'Smileys' or 'emoticons' have found uses for punctuation marks (#^%&*@$:...) that many people never knew existed, let alone used in writing. Sometimes they offer a crude visual substitute for words (e.g. (:-D = big mouth; _8_(l)___ = Homer Simpson), or they will convey the emotional subtext or tone of a text message: the kind of information that would be communicated, in normal conversation, by facial expressions and body language (e.g. *:-0 = alarmed;)l-[= tired and grumpy). According to Fast Company magazine, more than 2000 have been coined so far, since the moment in 1982 when Carnegie Mellon University researcher Scott Fahlman started labelling humorous comments on an early electronic bulletin board with a :-). Misconstrued sarcasm and irony were causing arguments to break out among posters. Twenty years later, irony is still causing US emailers serious problems. When despair.com registered :-(as a trademark and threatened to press charges against seven million email users for infringing their intellectual property rights, no one got the joke.

A product of ASCII's limitations, the emoticon will surely become a technological fossil of the late 20th century. More powerful computing will bring new opportunities for visual languages to develop, and for people to find their own unique style of graphic expression – their visual 'voice' – by increasingly knitting together text with pictorial elements. Visual communication is on the way to becoming universal; not in the sense of globally accepted signs or symbols, but in its application. Before long, it may be possible to write this way and be understood anywhere in the world. And if your visual vocabulary includes your local 'men at work' road sign, everyone will know where you're writing from, too.

UK cycle lane paintings

Application can be more interesting than theory. The British cycle lane symbol, signifying dedicated channels of road for cyclists, was first defined in the UK's Traffic Signs Regulations, 1982. As unambiguous as the original was (1215cm long, 750cm across), it has been open to interpretation by road sign painters and contractors ever since. Cycle any distance in London and you'll encounter all manner of contraptions and instruments of torture. Documented by designer Phil Carter, they turn the cycle lane into a gallery of bizarre tarmac art.

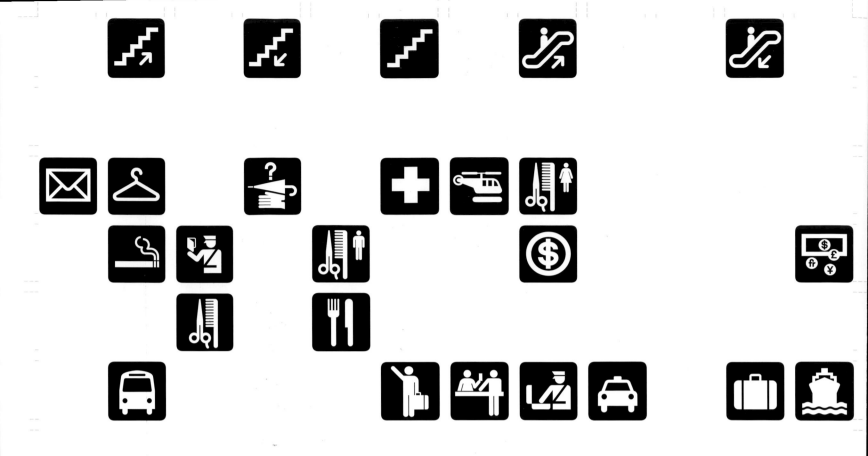

Public information signs, from the US, India and Japan

Public information sign systems tend to reflect and reinforce the cultural ideas that characterize a society. In India, pictorial signs are a must. Literacy is low and 14 different languages are spoken. Communication is further inhibited by traditional divisions between sexes, religions and castes. When a sign system was developed for Indian hospitals, it needed to reflect the shape of Indian society, and included signs for 'rural man', 'men's queue', 'ladies' queue', 'male doctor' and 'lady doctor'.

An associated system for transport facilities featured symbols for 'men's waiting room' and 'ladies' waiting room'.

The Japanese set reflects a national love of snow sports, traditional culture and courtesy.

WORDS

PIC0064 US Department of Transportation public information signs
PIC0065 Signs from Indian hospitals and transportation facilities
PIC0066 Japanese public information signs

082
083

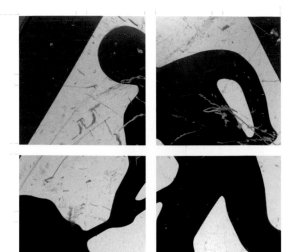

Deviations from standard road signs

While global corporations are able to enforce absolute conformity in their own systems of signs and insignia the world over, there is no universal guardian of signs that convey other, arguably more important information. These 'men at work' road signs from around the world highlight the cultural diversity to be found in the application of a widely accepted graphic standard. The stoop or straight back, the broad or emaciated trunk, the size of the mound and the effort being applied to it - nothing is quite the same in any two places.

Global 'men at work' signs

PIC00068

WORDS

WORDS

WORDS

086

087

Low-literacy healthcare pamphlets 1

An important tool in health education in countries where literacy levels are low is the pictorial pamphlet. To make health issues more relevant to local populations and to render medical procedures less alarming, these typically tell a story in pictures of ordinary people, reflect local customs, dress, etc. and employ a local style of illustration. Infant healthcare and forms of birth control are common subjects. Clocks, calendars, night and day are used to indicate the passage of time.

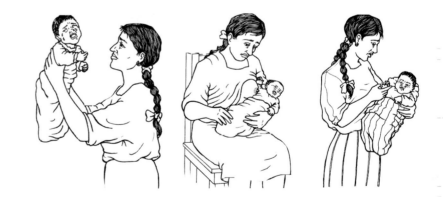

Low-literacy healthcare pamphlets 2

From Guatemala, a leaflet on childbirth and childcare, with a less than happy ending.

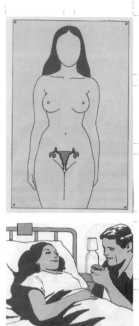

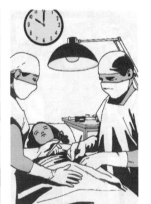

Low-literacy healthcare pamphlets 3

A colour leaflet from El Salvador on female sterilization, concentrating on the painlessness and speed of the procedure, not to mention its worth as a topic of male conversation.

US aerial propaganda - Operation Desert Storm

Some of these drawings may look like the work of a war-obsessed 14 year old but the crude, hand-drawn style was calculated by the Central Intelligence Agency's Psychological Operations (PSYOPS) Division to have maximum impact on the morale of Iraqi troop lines during the Gulf War. The message was stark: fight and die for sure, or surrender and see your family again. Combined with terrifying reports of the allied bombing campaign, the leaflets were highly effective in destroying Iraqi fighting spirit.

US aerial propaganda – Afghanistan

A decade later, the target for PSYCPS was the Afghan civilian. A 70% illiteracy rate demanded a campaign of largely pictorial material. A leaflet with colour, computer-generated illustrations was dropped, showing how to feed a family on the humanitarian daily rations being distributed simultaneously.

i-mode website icons 1

How do you fit a website on a mobile phone screen? In Japan, NTT DoCoMo's hugely successful i-mode network allows subscribers to access more than 40,000 websites. To aid site-owners in creating i-mode compatible versions of the r sites, NTT DoCoMo developed a set of 180 'emoji' icons - visual shorthand for constructing information, menus, ads and links.

US aerial propaganda - Operation Desert Storm

Some of these drawings may look like the work of a war-obsessed 14 year old but the crude, hand-drawn style was calculated by the Central Intelligence Agency's Psychological Operations (PSYOPS) Division to have maximum impact on the morale of Iraqi troop lines during the Gulf War. The message was stark: fight and die for sure, or surrender and see your family again. Combined with terrifying reports of the allied bombing campaign, the leaflets were highly effective in destroying Iraqi fighting spirit.

US aerial propaganda – Afghanistan

A decade later, the target for PSYOPS was the Afghan civilian. A 70% illiteracy rate demanded a campaign of largely pictorial material. A leaflet with colour, computer-generated illustrations was dropped, showing how to feed a family on the humanitarian daily rations being distributed simultaneously.

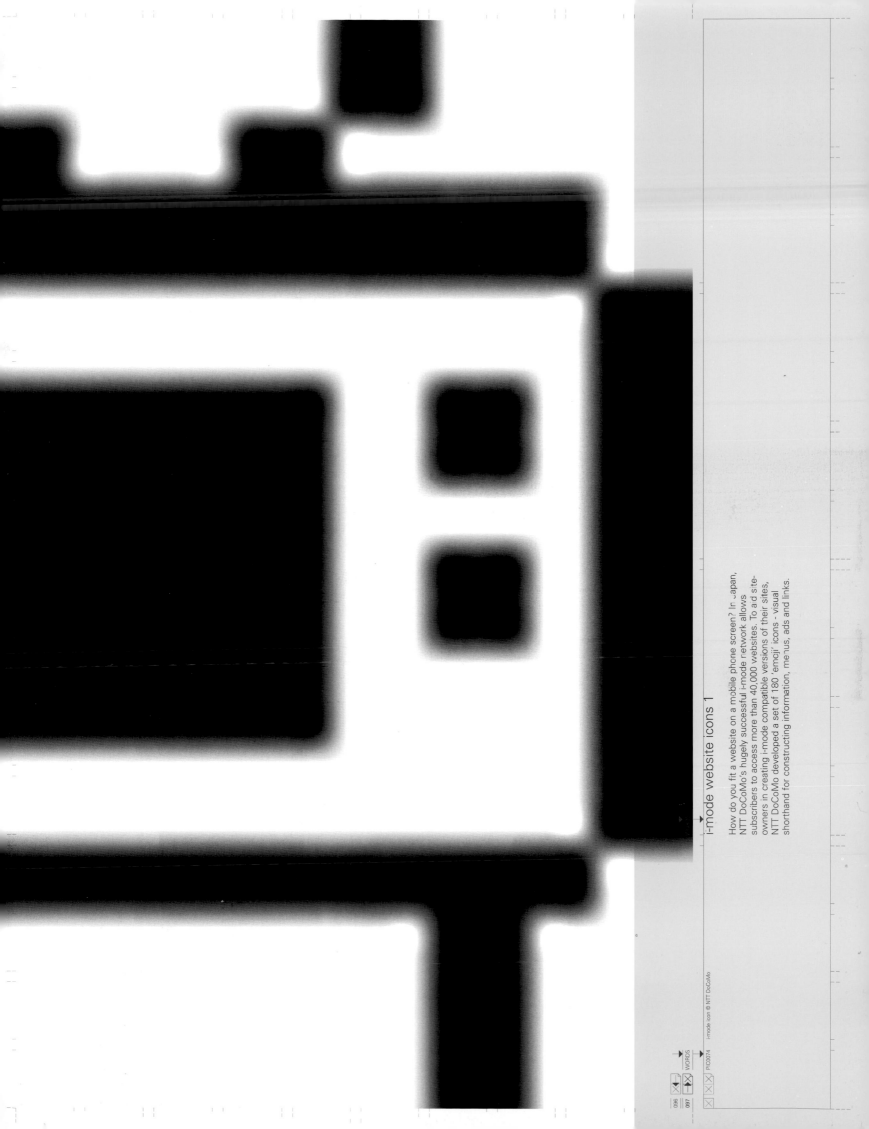

i-mode website icons 1

How do you fit a website on a mobile phone screen? In Japan, NTT DoCoMo's hugely successful i-mode network allows subscribers to access more than 40,000 websites. To aid site-owners in creating i-mode compatible versions of their sites, NTT DoCoMo developed a set of 180 'emoji' icons - visual shorthand for constructing information, menus, ads and links.

i-mode website icons 2

The icons occupy a mere 12x12 pixels each, and yet are able to represent a whole range of concepts most commonly used by online services: types of weather, starsigns sports, modes of transport, shops, pastimes, moods and so on.

i-mode icons © NTT DoCoMo

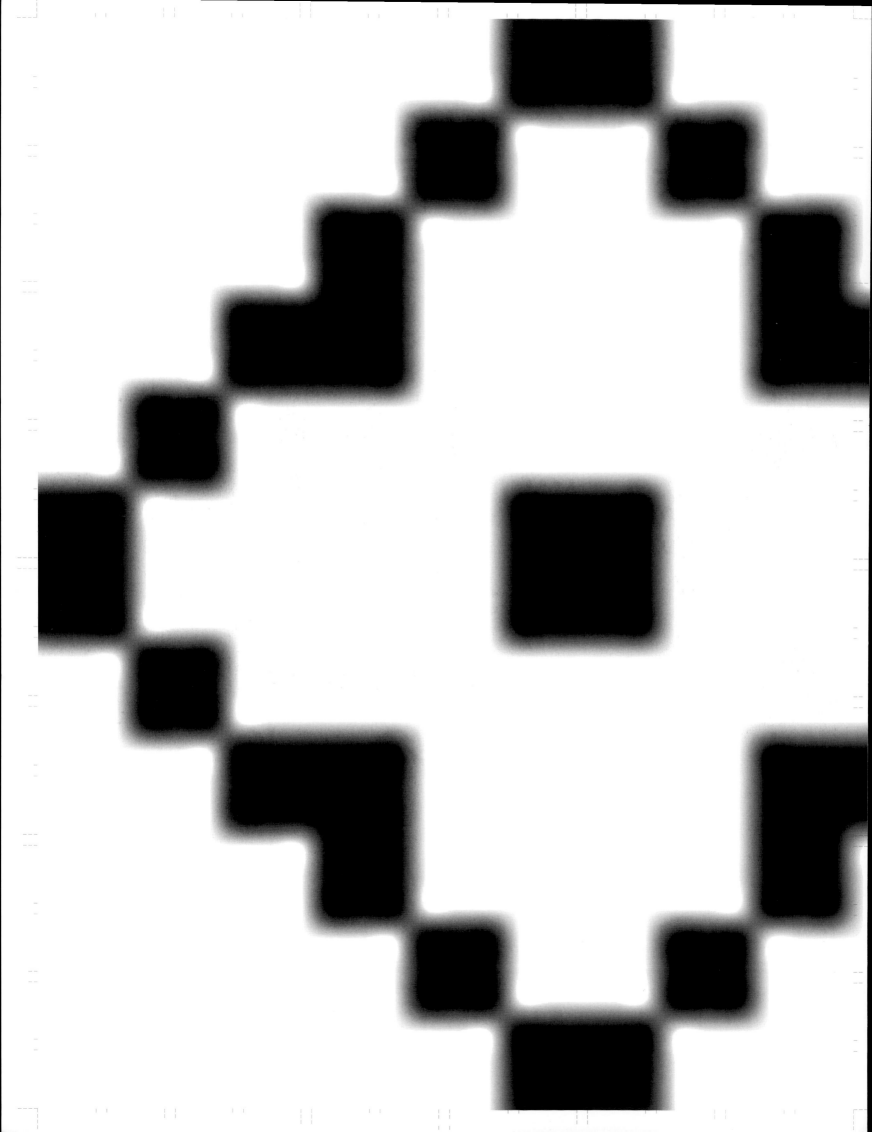

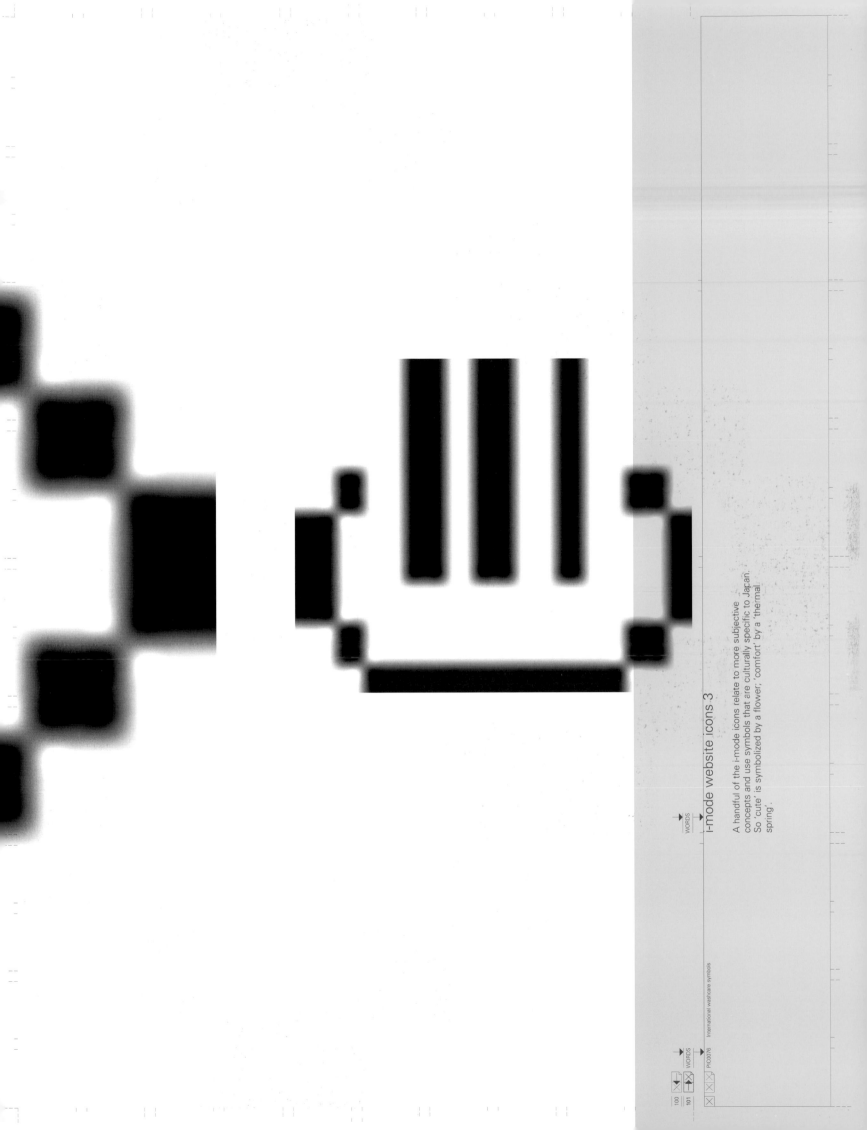

i-mode website icons 3

A handful of the i-mode icons relate to more subjective concepts and use symbols that are culturally specific to Japan. So 'cute' is symbolized by a flower; 'comfort' by a 'thermal spring'.

WORDS

PIC0076

International washcare symbols

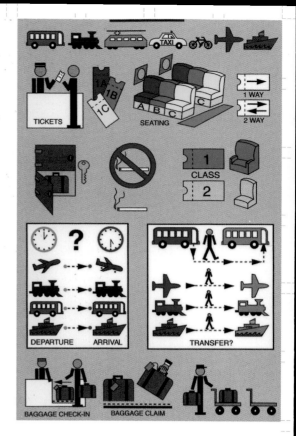

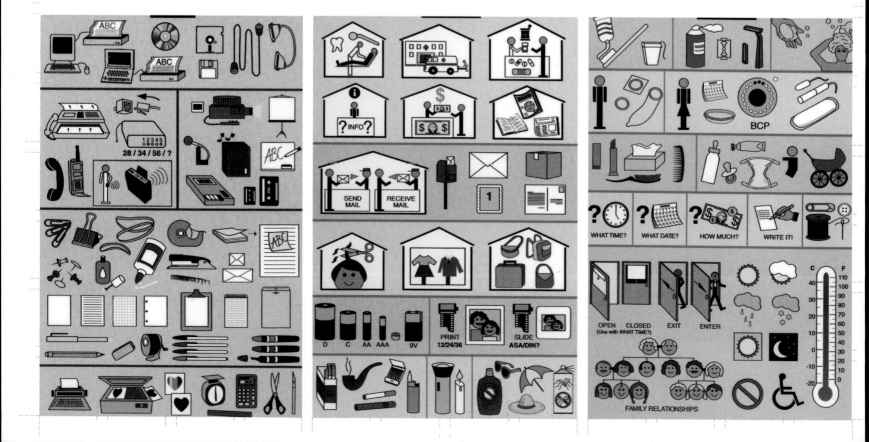

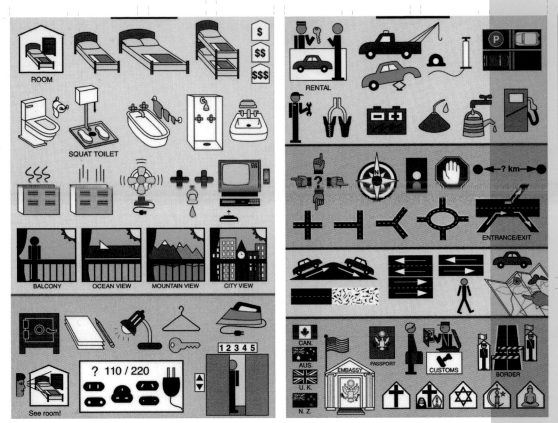

Kwikpoint International Translator

Human survival boiled down to a few hundred icons. Pocket translators like Kwikpoint are improving cross–cultural communication no end; they could even kill off the notoriously feeble attempts of British and American tourists to communicate in languages other than their own. Developed by Alan Stillman, a Washington computer system's analyst, after being stuck for words on holiday in Hungary, Kwikpoint is a double-sided picture card with 600 illustrations designed to help monolinguists get by anywhere in the world: they simply point to the relevant picture(s) on the card. Advice from linguists, anthropologists and diplomats aided the selection of images, which cover everything from buying food, medicine or contraceptives to requesting a sea view, a squat toilet or the fire brigade.

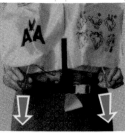

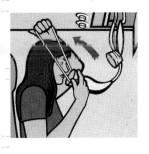

Flight safety instructions

From aircraft to aircraft, airline to airline, the information these cards convey is always the same and it is always conveyed with as few words as possible. The style often echoes that of instructions for home assembly furniture – impersonal, mechanical and wholly unrealistic – and yet there is still enormous variety to be found in the quality of illustration and the quality of information, as these comparisons show. A lot might be read into these instructions as to how highly each airline rates the safety of its passengers. Alternatively, since the concept of emergency instructions is almost totally redundant – how many people in crashing planes will actually consult one of these? – perhaps they should just serve to show how utopian graphic communication can be.

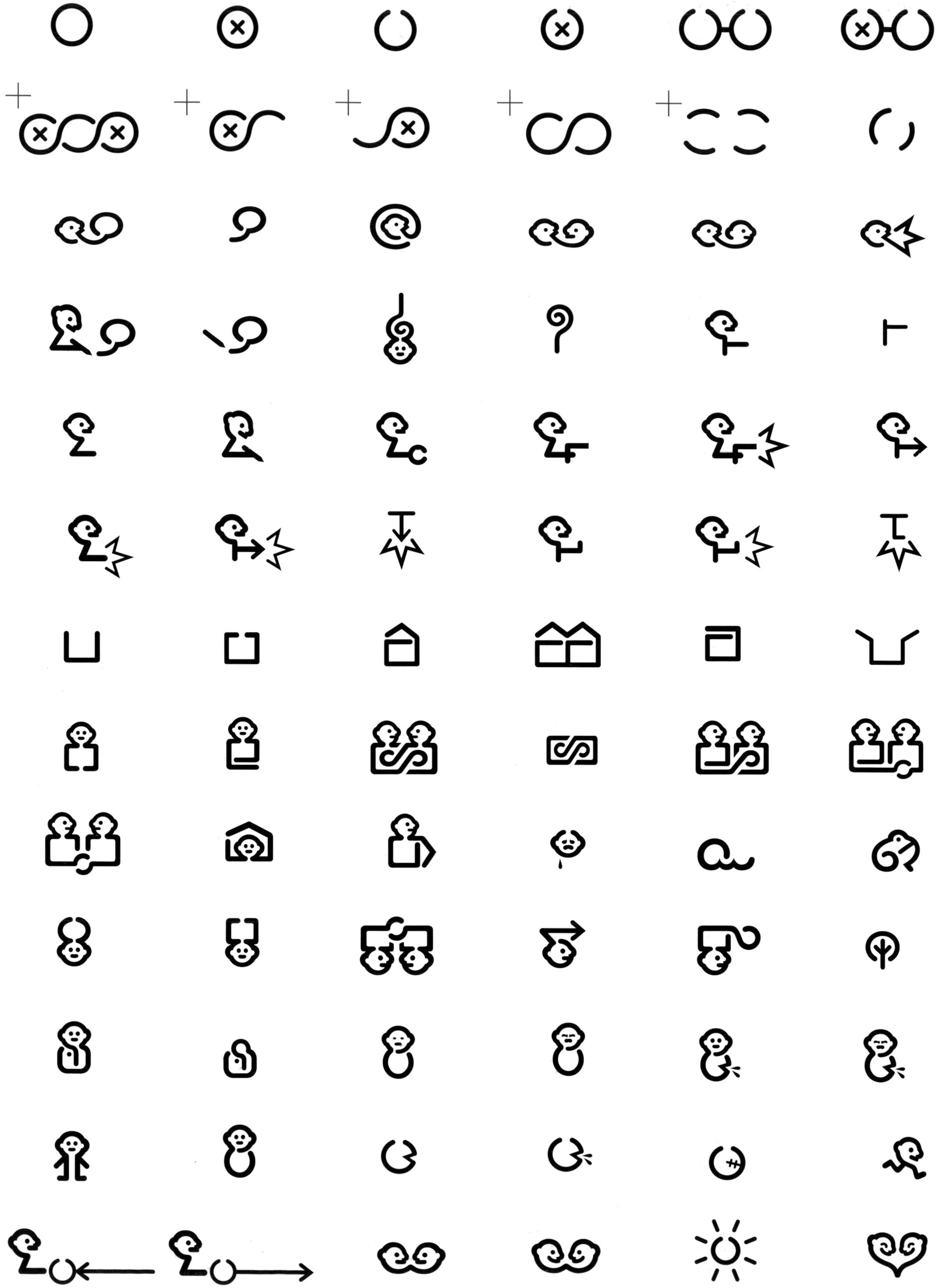

The Elephant's Memory

One of the grails of cross-cultural graphic communication is a visual language that would ultimately replace the written word and allow individuals of any nationality to communicate freely. An unusually polished attempt to create a pictorial language, 'The Elephant's Memory' by Timothee Ingen-Housz, consists of a vocabulary of 150 combinable logograms representing concepts such as time, existence, causality and so on. These signs 'snap' together to form sentences that could, in turn, be fleshed out electronically with other media such as a movie file or an image. The name of the system acknowledges the fact that large numbers of people would need to learn and remember the pictorial language for it to catch on. However, Ingen-Housz's dream is of a 'living language' that individuals can improvise with and create dialects from.

The Elephant's Memory by Timothee Ingen-Housz (from left to right, top to bottom): all; nothing; to be/no; to be with; to be with out; all but; nothing but; to be; maybe; before/after; future; life/death; birth; death; causality; if/then; maybe; field; light; one; several; a few; to speak; language; me; you; someone; to shout; writing; to wonder; interrogation; to point at; determiner; these; to name; name; to be scared (horror); to be stunned (scry); to do; to trace; to hold; to point at (gun); to shoot at; to create; freeform; to use; tool; gun; to eat; to hit; to direct; "don't"; "stop !!!"; "don't" !!!; to refuse; to hide; to be happy; receptacle; box; house/shelter; village; closed; open; envelop; etc; to be down; to be surprised (happy); day; to be angry; to have; to possess; to exchange; money; to send; to give; car; to lend/to loan; night; to get; to pass on; to live in; to protect; to cry; ocean; frog; rabbit; bird; elephant; to sleep; to be tired; to think; to know (information); to pass on information; intention; to get information; tree; forest; leaf; female genitalia; male genitalia; out; copulation; to be clothed; cloth; to be sick; to suffer from...; to bleed; to be wounded; body damaged; to leak; fixed; to run; to walk; to hear; to see; to hate; to cry; to receive; to send; acquaintance; friendship; sun; determiner; love; early love; relationship; love relationship; hate relationship;

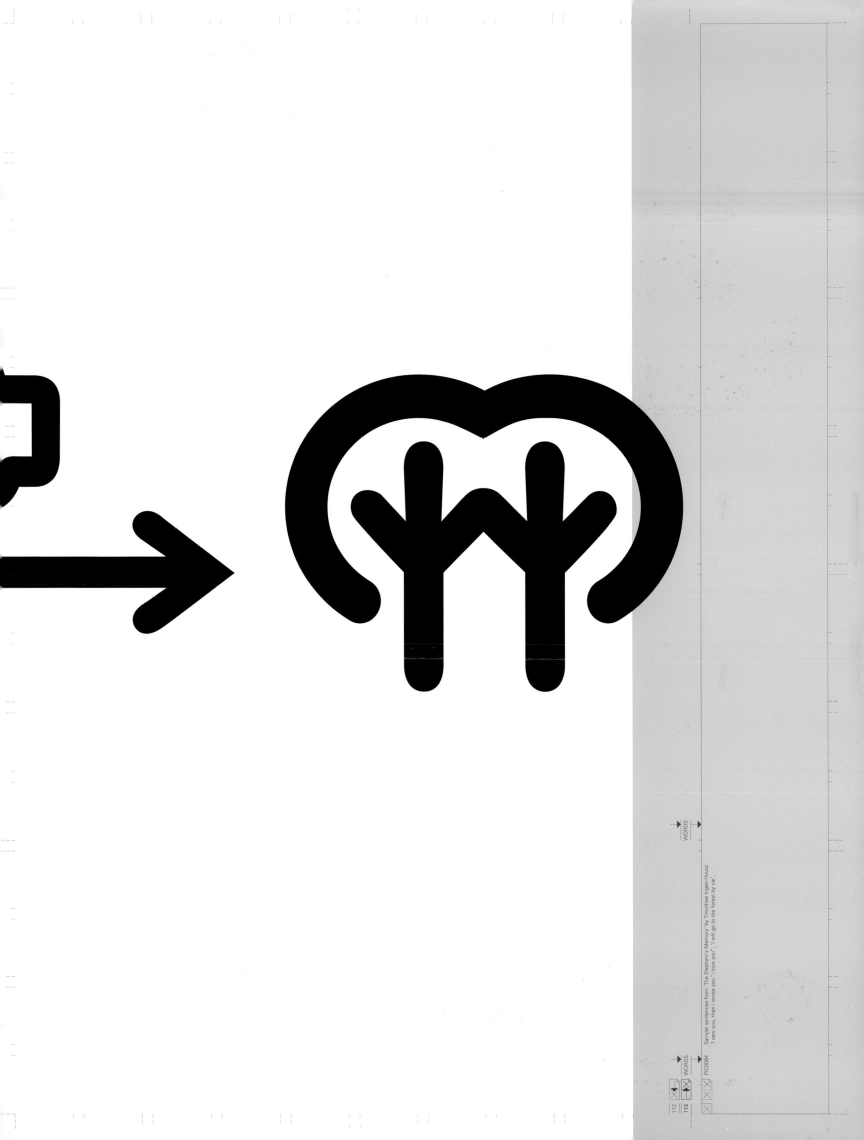

Sample sentences from 'The Elephant's Memory' by Timothee Ingen-Housz
'I saw you, then i wrote you.' 'I love you.' 'I will go to the forest by car'.

津波避難所
Tsunami Evacuation

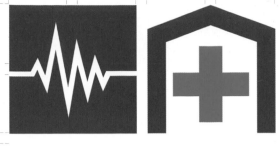

PICO085   Tsunami warning sign system developed by GK Kyoto Inc and Professor Haruo
           Hayashi of the Disaster Prevention Institute of Kyoto University

WORDS

Tsunami warning sign system

A growing, more mobile population is one more vulnerable to disasters, we are told by the developers of Japan's new tsunami warning sign system. You can see their point. Go for a holiday on Shikoku Island and you might not realize that every 100 years earthquakes trigger devastating tidal waves several storeys high. Signboards at the railway station and the harbour inform the visitor of the hazard and of the warning and evacuation system. Pictograms are combined, mirroring kanji (Chinese character) formation, to create visual phrases and wordless directions. Not great for the tourist industry, maybe, but at least the tourists will know where to take cover.

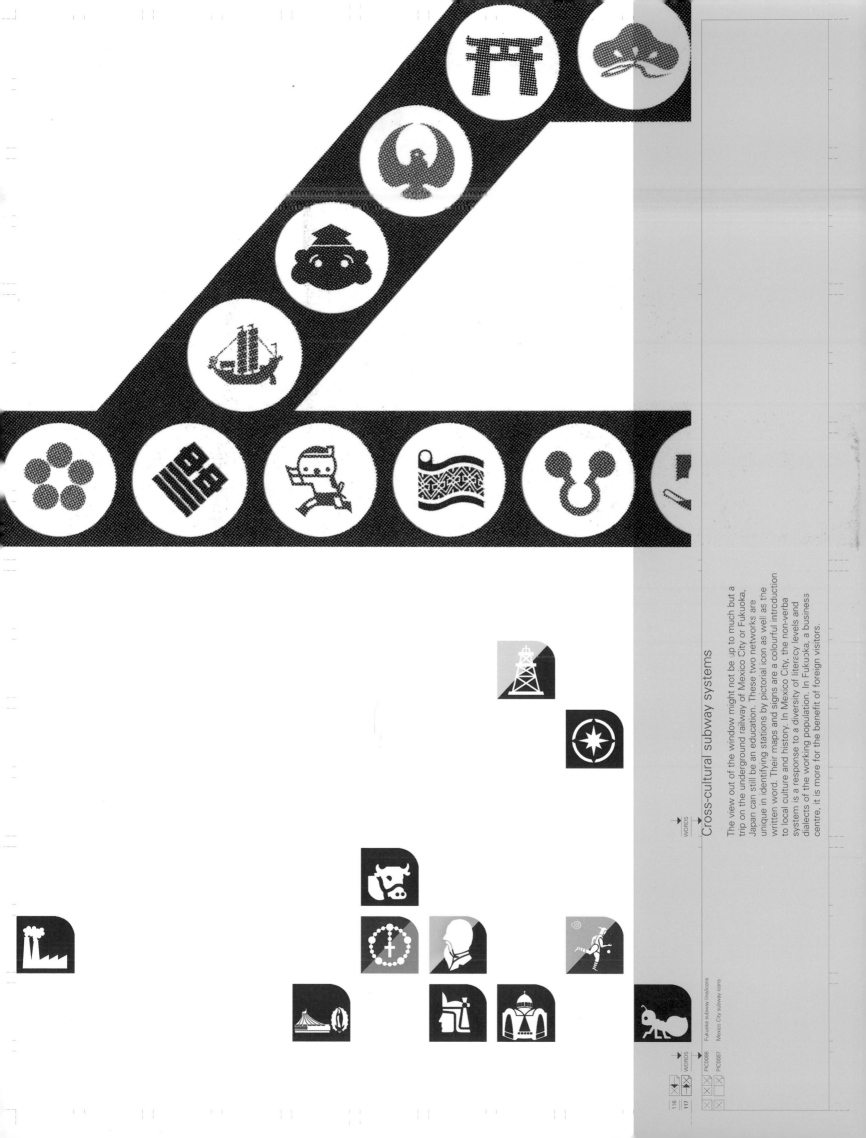

Cross-cultural subway systems

The view out of the window might not be up to much but a trip on the underground railway of Mexico City or Fukuoka, Japan can still be an education. These two networks are unique in identifying stations by pictorial icon as well as the written word. Their maps and signs are a colourful introduction to local culture and history. In Mexico City, the non-verbal system is a response to a diversity of literacy levels and dialects of the working population. In Fukuoka, a business centre, it is more for the benefit of foreign visitors.

WORDS

Fukuoka subway lines/icons

Mexico City subway icons

116

117

PIC0086

PIC0087

@>--;-- O:-) 0*-) d:-) :-)
:-)8< (((H))) :-X =|:o} (:-D
(=) :-E :-F }|{ })i({ }:-X o
<):o) :-S H-) :`-(:(:-@
:#) .\/ <:-I :-6 5:-) :") >
W :^{= /:-) 8) %-) |^o (
%*@:-(?:^[] (8{ @:-} :-x
(-: >;-> 8:-) |-(X-(&-I
) :) :-{ :-3 :-#):-(8-O :
3:[}:^#) +<:-) :-t +:-) X
{= :-C ([([:] 3:*> :(:-d
(~:-P :-/ O-) ;^) :-i :-?
:-a <:>== =):-) :-\ |:-) :-
:-{}]-I {:-) :-" '-) ,-) 8<:
=8-0 $-)

) :~-(: = , :-)^< (:-)

?-(:-] :-}X %-6 :-

) C=:-) 8^ ;-(:-.)

O-) >:-> :-e :3-] :*)

>-) |:-O :-! =:-H :-

8^(|) (_8(|) *^_^*

-* >^,,^< >:-I @(*0*)@

(*) :-S @@@@:-) 8(:-

:^) 3:] :8) :--) P-(

) =:-) =:-(:-r (((((:-

<|:-) :-> :-@ $__$ +-

-Q :-(<| %-) :-0 :-&

(:-(:-< [:-) 8-) B-)

-=#:-) \ ,-} |-O :-(0)

The original email 'smiley' was conceived in the early 1980s as a
way of using keyboard characters to indicate the tone of a text
comment, or the state of mind of the sender. It has mutated into a
visual vocabulary, incorporating ever more obscure additions. The
'emoticon', as it is sometimes known, is evidence of individuals
wishing to express themselves visually. It will become obsolete as
computing power increases, but could be replaced by clip-art of
much greater variety and finish, allowing users to weave together
text and pictures as they type, in more integrated fashion

Utopian simplicity

In 1992, in a collection of essays by architects, designers, critics and scholars called The Edge of the Millennium (Watson-Guptill Publications), Ellen Lupton and J. Abbott Miller contributed a characteristically astute study of 'the hieroglyphics of communication': the 'tidy icons' that dominate modern experience, such as public information signs, corporate logotypes and newspaper 'infographics'. The essay became one of the inspirations for this book. Towards the end of it, Lupton and Miller issued an appeal. 'If graphic design provides an interface between people and products, could it not also provide an interface between people and culture? We call this utopian project for design in the next millennium "critical wayfinding," or the construction of interfaces that serve not to package corporate messages but rather to provide alternate routes of access to media and information.'

On the evidence presented by this book, that interface 'between people and products' has been ground down in many cases to a single, wordless, worldwide image. The 'critical wayfinding' of today, if it is to gain our attention and beckon us behind the curtain of corporate hype and political spin, must be as iconic and powerful and cross-cultural as the smartest global branding campaign or international standard symbol.

World Without Words ends by visiting the work of some of the artists and activists who are rising to this challenge. Operating outside the spheres of government, commerce and regulation that dominate the rest of this book, they have co-opted the visual information formats and tools of those worlds to reflect new truths and realities back at us, and reflect them back with a wordless, cultureless intensity that demands we stop and think.

Writing with images

Few publications or pieces of design have made us stop and think quite like number 13 of Colors magazine. Colors, said its founding editor-in-chief Tibor Kalman, was 'inspired by the age of instant communication'. It was 'about the ways in which we are all similar, yet celebrates our differences'. Published by knitwear brand Benetton, it sold around 500,000 copies globally, and was determinedly low on text. 'Colors writes with images,' said Kalman. 'We think pictures cross borders, reach more people, convey more information and make a bigger impact than words alone.'

In December 1995, the 'world's first truly global magazine' published its 13th edition – 'the first ever magazine without words'. Kalman's final issue in charge, Colors 13 was a rush of uncaptioned news and stock photo library pictures. 'I've always been frustrated by language and I wanted to see if we could create something visual that went beyond it. So [Colors 13] can be enjoyed in virtually the same way by a person in Vietnam as by a person in Uzbekistan or New York.' Each spread was a visual essay carefully composed to show all sides of a topic. The images

standardization of media images, throwing regulation stick figures into the full gamut of human interactions. Scenes from brutal down-the-page news stories are played out by figures whose lives have until now been lived out on toilet doors, airport signs and fast-food packaging. 'I love them,' said Massimo Vignelli. 'I suddenly want them to have a name. Or perhaps they should not since they are universal, above and beyond races, nationalities and context.' However, working with such a reduced visual language creates its own rigid discipline. 'Making an almost self-evident image is very difficult,' says Lionni. 'There is no method, the process isn't rational – I just do it until it either works or I get fed up. The list of image-resistant ideas is endless.'

What is real, what is artificial? How much should we feel about what we see on TV, what we read? Lionni attempts to get us closer to reality. But whereas Lionni is exposing public reality, the American artist Matt Mullican reveals a more personal, confidential kind of reality. His bold, colour-coded pictographic signs, based closely on those found at airports, are often pointers to private universes, trails of memorabilia and artefacts. They seem to mimic the way we think about such signs: universal symbols activating streams of private mental symbols. In other works, Mullican animates the Isotype man of the standard public information sign. He gives him a degree of life and emotional intelligence, and we automatically flesh out the rest of his character.

'Up to 625' is a web-based work (www.centreimage. ch/mullican), produced for Documenta X in Kassel in 1998, which extended Mullican's work with pictograms, mental maps and memories into the realm of interactive media. The screen is divided into five zones of different colour. Click on one and a set of symbols appears, each one a doorway to a separate, complex system of references: patterns and textures, insects, the 1967 World's Fair, comic book excerpts, invented pictograms and virtual spaces.

From a moment in 1978 when, grounded in a Nova Scotia airport, he first became aware of the ubiquity and iconic charge of the reduced public signs around him, Mullican has been constructing his private wordless worlds. 'I'm just trying to diagram what we have in us,' he has said. It sounds such a modest undertaking. But if there is one thing that Mullican and all the other contributors to the following pages have in common, it is their desire to represent the complex with the simple. In fact, the same thing unites everything in this book; it is just that the scale of that complexity – the ambition of the work – is greatest in this final chapter. A sign tells us where to go. A logo pretends it is simplifying something complex for us when it actually represents something terribly ordinary: running shoes, oil or toothpaste. The designers, artists and activists here have sought inspiration from less mediated, everyday experiences to reveal important, difficult truths about the world we live in. If there is any real value in a world without words, this is it.

attempted hits in 24 hours. The opportunities for designing eco-information for local communities in ways that are engaging, quick to grasp and culturally in tune are only just starting to be explored. The Green Map System (GMS) offers eco-information of a different kind to Scorecard, but in a form that is just as succinct and universally adaptable. Graphic designer Wendy Brawer published the first Green Map in her home town of New York City, as a way of guiding tourists and local residents towards an involvement with green initiatives. Since 1996, with the collaboration of a global group of like-minded designers, Brawer has turned the GMS into an award-winning shared visual language – a set of 125 icons that symbolize different kinds of green site and cultural resources, from markets, cafés, gardens and museums to renewable resources sites, wildlife habitats and places of natural beauty. It also maps 'toxic hotspots': traffic hazards, pollution sources and waste sites. Mapmakers around the world, once they have registered with www.greenmap.com and agreed to a set of standards, have been left free to download the digitized icon set and publish their own, regionally flavoured versions that fulfil their community's local needs.

It's an extraordinary demonstration of how symbol design, new media and a liberal attitude to intellectual property can enable 'critical wayfinding' at a local level. By September 2002, 107 Green Maps in 37 countries on all inhabited continents had been completed. No two are alike – in fact, the diversity in the visual texture of the maps is astonishing – and yet the adherence of each one to a consistent set of icons means that cities can be fairly compared. Together, they offer a powerful picture of how urban centres from Mexico City to Port Elizabeth to St Petersburg to Hiroshima are making progress towards ecological and cultural sustainability.

Technology is handing individuals the tools to generate and disseminate powerful cross-cultural graphic communication. While studying at Cologne's Academy of Media Arts, Timothee Ingen-Housz was able to develop a unique, non-linear pictorial language, consisting of over 150 'logograms'. Rather than simply suggest visual equivalents for words and phrases, these logograms represent concepts, such as time, causality, existence and so on, that can be combined to form 'sentences'. 'The Elephant's Memory', as he called it, was designed to be refined in 'language kitchens': virtual, collaborative, educational environments in which people from various cultural backgrounds would be invited to explore this new means of communication.

One of the things that makes 'The Elephant's Memory' unique is its visual finish. Logograms are rounded, friendly and attractive to children, but they are also designed to be reproduced at every scale and in every medium. However, adds Ingen-Housz, this is a living language: 'they are meant to be reproduced by hand and give birth to handwritten dialects all over the world.... Drawn in sand or snow, tagged on a wall or carved in wood, they jump out of the screen and invade the real world.'

were mundane, troubling, bizarre and brutal and their juxtapositions were, in many instances, unforgettable. The contrasts were those a fact-finding extraterrestrial might make. What is eating? Colors showed people doing it with their hands, their feet, with tools and syringes. What is aggression? Colors found it on the faces of football supporters, Serbian soldiers and stockbrokers.

Colors 13 ran up heavy bills with photo agencies but it had discovered a new way of presenting information. In the words of one critic, Kalman had 'evolved a design language that functioned on a global level, by allowing a culturally diverse readership to contemplate both the particular and universal concept'.

The same could be said of The State of the World Atlas, produced by Myriad Editions in the UK for Penguin Books. Presenting enormous amounts of information about political, economic and social trends across the world, this visual survey employs maps in which data is multidimensional. By assigning a variable to the size that countries have on each map, as well as one to their colour, we get an immediate global view of how food, arms, manufacturing, refugees, tobacco, child labour, illiteracy and a host of other neglected measurables are shared out by the world's nations. 'These are the bad dreams of the modern world, given color and shape and submitted to a grid that can be grasped instantaneously,' said the New York Times. The LA Times called The State of the World Atlas 'Unique and uniquely beautiful'. 'A single map here tells us more about the world today than a dozen statistical abstracts or scholarly tomes.'

Online, www.scorecard.org is a superb example of how graphic information can serve 'right-to-know' movements. On its homepage is a small, text-free map of the US with what looks like a bad attack of the measles, especially in the eastern states. The gestalt it creates is so powerful, you have to investigate. It turns out that this is a distribution of 'toxic releases from industrial facilities'. There's a list of other 'environmental maps': 'lead hazards', 'land contamination', 'animal waste from factory farms', and so on.

Scorecard does little more than present official statistics in a highly visual, condensed form. But features such as a 'type in your zip code' approach to checking the local pollution picture have led to major web traffic through the site. When it was launched in April 1998 by Environmental Defense, it received an overwhelming response: one million hits and

Storytelling by signs

That kind of invitation, to appropriate, reinterpret and reinvent established visual languages, was never extended by the creators of road signs and public information symbols. Nevertheless, the graphic infrastructure of our lives is providing contemporary artists with visual materials that are culturally neutral and have a ready-made place in the popular consciousness. The contradictions, gaps, ambiguities, repetitions and familiarity of so many signs present a mental environment in which the artist can play with our assumptions and disturb our 'relationship to these silent, silhouetted figures.

For many, our apparent submission to a handful of standardized symbols and sign formats is something to be questioned. 'We'd like to dissolve certain boundaries which have been rigidly established in people, to shatter the monotony and mundanity which many people feel trapped in,' say the anonymous members of the Interdimensional Pixie Broadcast Network (IPBN) who, on August 31 2000, staged a minor situationist coup in Exeter, south-west England, placing a number of invented warning signs at roadsides around the city. These ranged from the amusing (signs that warned of 'fairies', 'blobs' and 'snails', or replaced the exclamation mark [danger] sign with other, more equivocal punctuation marks), to the mystifying (ancient Celtic and Tibetan symbols).

'The red triangle is a sort of window into a world of authority. When a driver sees a black symbol on a white background in a red triangle on a pole by the side of the road, their mind automatically switches into a receptive state. Imagine if we were to spray symbols on to walls, graffiti-style. Most people would automatically filter these out. We want to bypass these filters. It's similar to computer hacking, in some ways. We're "hacking" an infrastructure of symbol/response which operates between the authorities and the public.' Precisely executed, many of the signs went unnoticed by drivers until a local radio station latched on to the story. By the evening the signs had disappeared, seized by fans and the local police force.

In his Facts of Life books and in exhibitions such as 'Primetime' (June 2002, Galerie Frédéric Giroux, Paris), Pippo Lionni is another who taps into our Pavlovian relationship to many everyday symbols. Lionni uses the language of industrial signs to criticize the

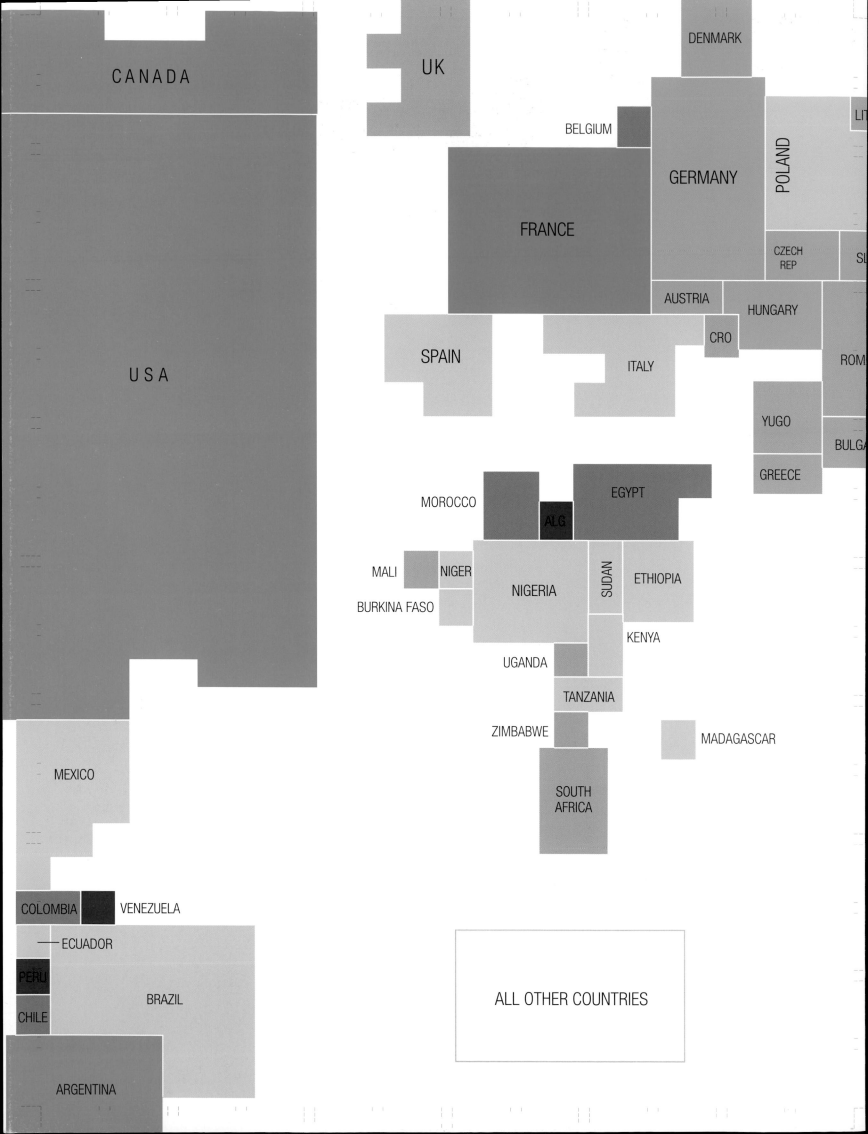

CANADA

UK

DENMARK

BELGIUM

GERMANY

POLAND

LIT

USA

FRANCE

CZECH
REP

SL

AUSTRIA

HUNGARY

CRO

SPAIN

ITALY

ROM

YUGO

BULGA

GREECE

MOROCCO

EGYPT

ALG.

MALI

NIGER

SUDAN

ETHIOPIA

NIGERIA

BURKINA FASO

KENYA

UGANDA

TANZANIA

ZIMBABWE

MADAGASCAR

MEXICO

SOUTH
AFRICA

COLOMBIA

VENEZUELA

ECUADOR

PERU

BRAZIL

ALL OTHER COUNTRIES

CHILE

ARGENTINA

State of the World Atlas

Data doesn't belong in lists; the only way to understand it is to see it. Now in its sixth edition, the State of the World Atlas (published by Penguin in the UK and US) takes raw data about the most important issues facing the planet and creates maps from it. Colour and area denote two separate variables, revealing at a glance the world's hotspots for pollution, food shortages, military might, refugees, consumerism, population growth and so on.

WORDS

WORDS

Military Spending: Food
Maps © Myriad Editions Ltd

PICCO30

124
125

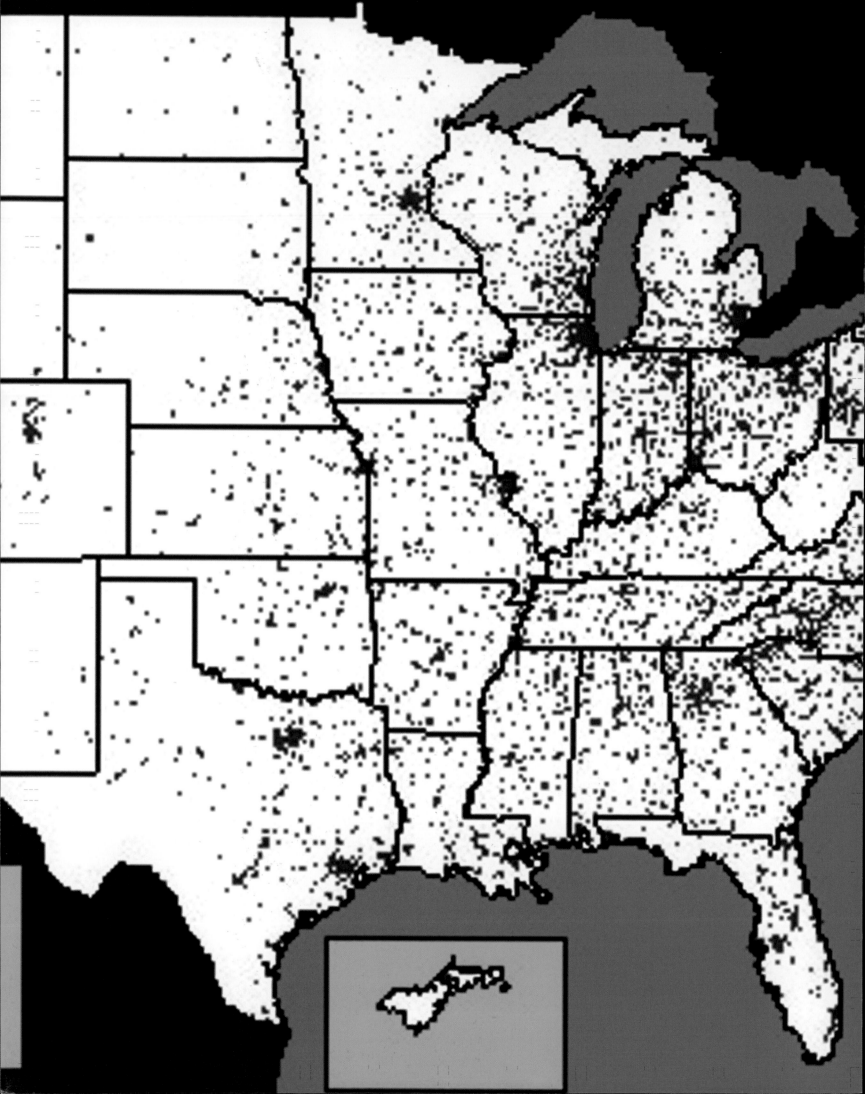

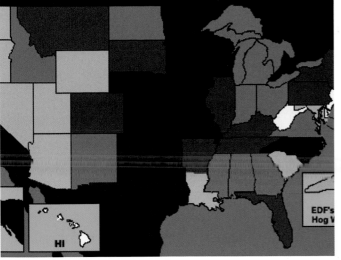

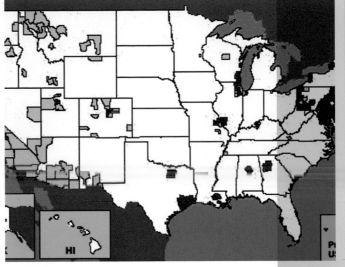

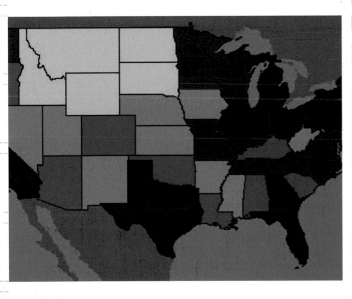

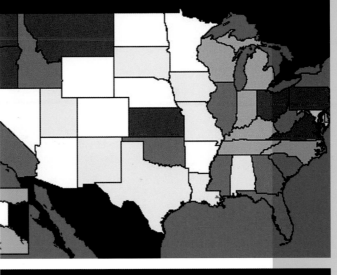

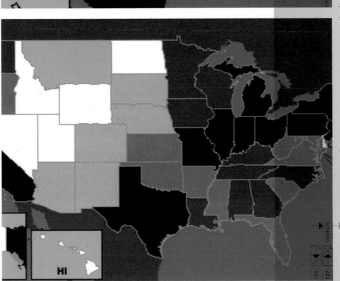

Scorecard

Visual information as shock tactics. Scorecard.org offers a massive prod in the ribs to anyone (in the US) who thinks environmental issues are somehow no longer a concern. On its home page, a series of maps highlight the national state of affairs on air pollutants, animal waste, industrial toxic releases and a range of other environmental criteria. These attention-grabbing maps demand to be explored; they pull you into the website. The most popular feature is a 'type-your-own-zipcode' approach to finding local information on environmental

conditions. In the same way a directory website will find you a local plumber or locksmith, scorecard.com will give you the latest on lead hazards or water purity in your area.

Opposite page: toxic releases from industrial facilities.
This page, left, from top to bottom: animal waste from factory farms (dark brown = worst offenders); hazardous air pollutants (red = greatest risk of cancer· from HAPs)

This page, right, from top to bottom: air pollutants (red = non-attainment of air quality standards); Clean Water Act status (green = most 'impaired water bodies'); watershed health (red

= poorest quality; lead hazards (dark grey = highest risk of lead hazard in housing)

EDF's
Hog W

www.scorecard.org © Environmental Defense, 2002

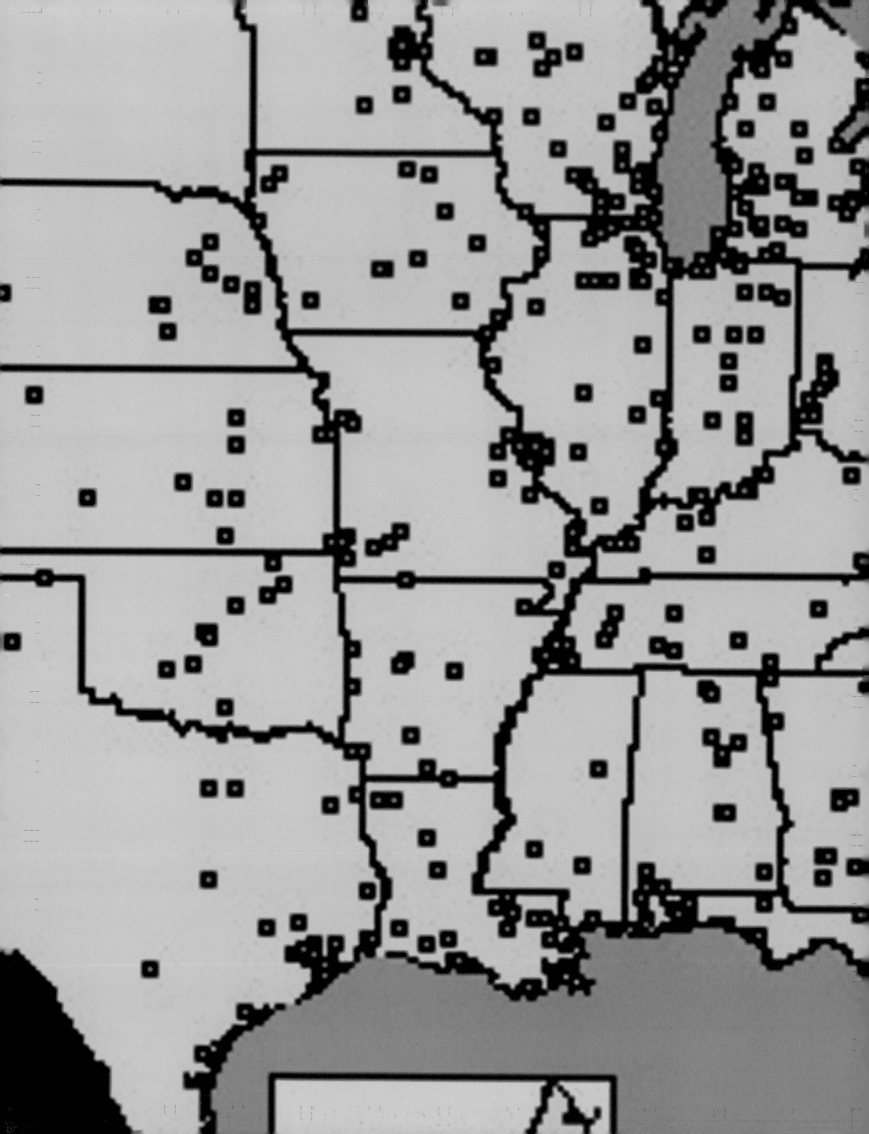

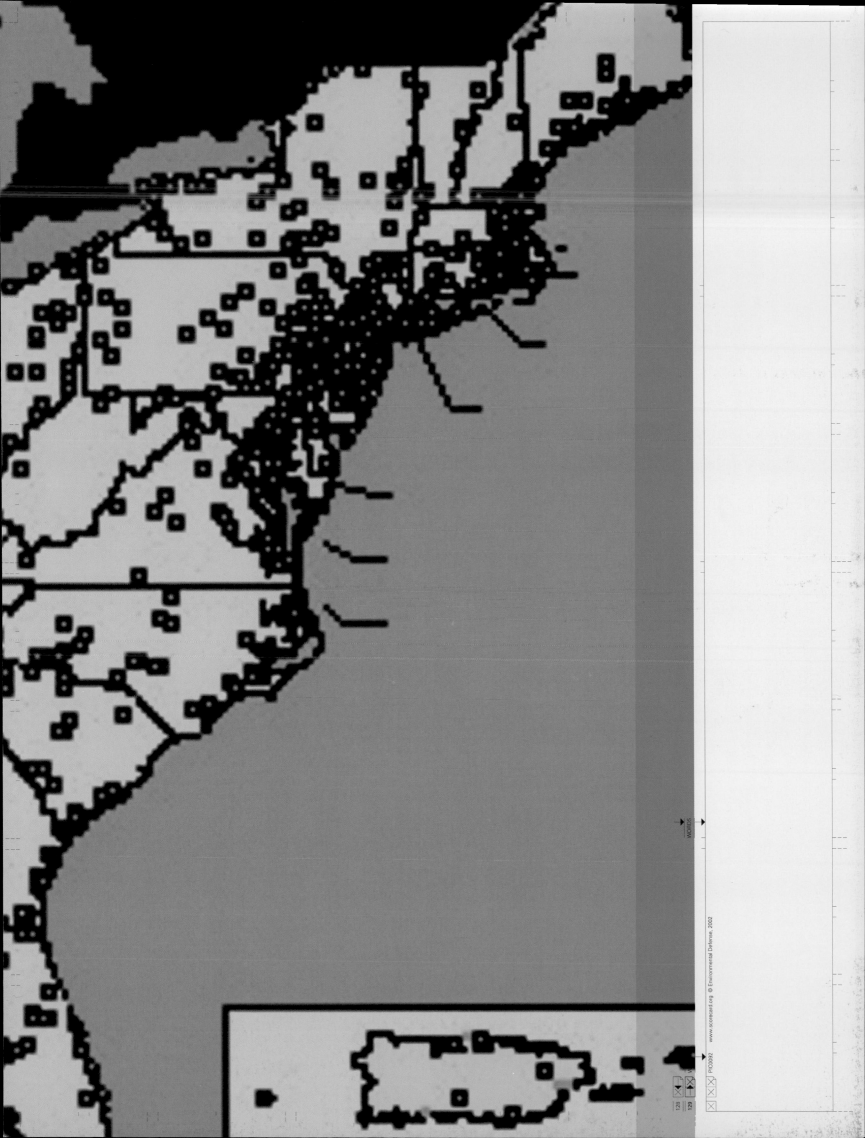

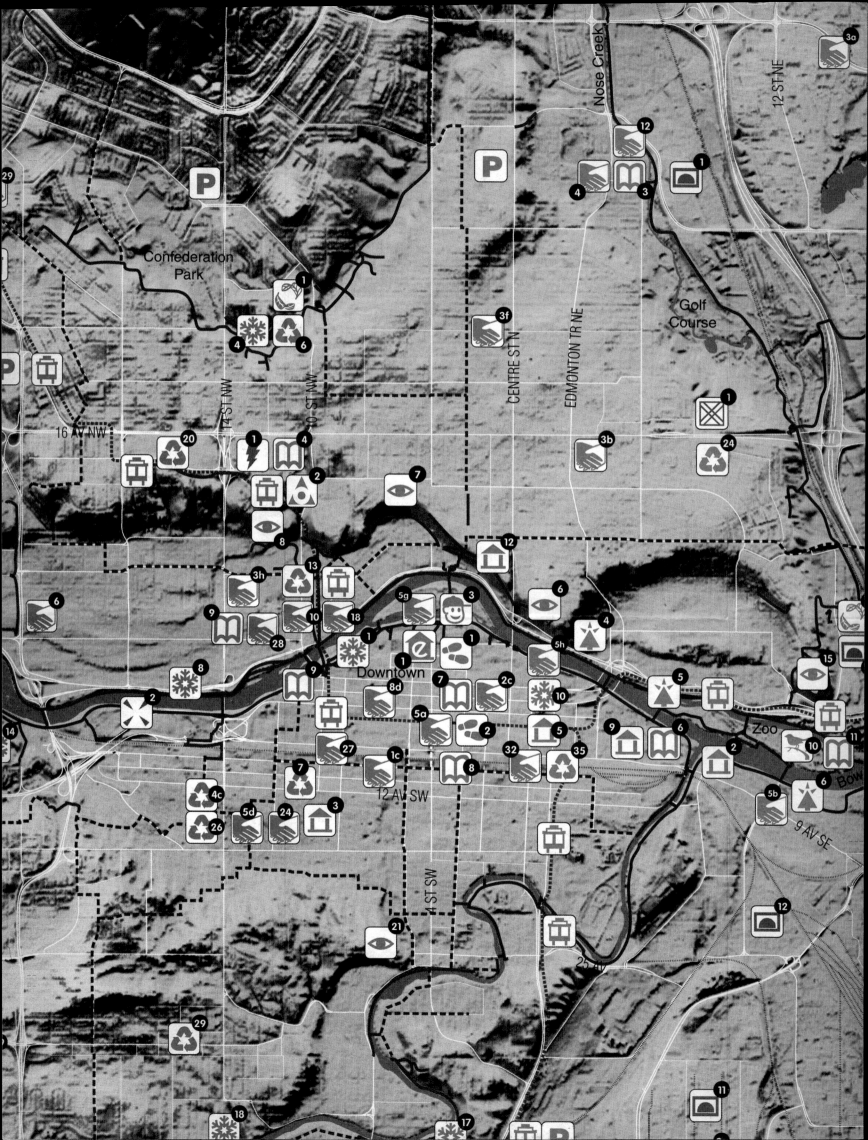

うめがおか

451

001 402

305

002

304

Green Maps

The Green Map System is an extraordinary coming together of activism, technology and design. When graphic designer Wendy Brawer created a map to show the location of environmental destinations and resources in her home town of New York City, she hardly expected to inspire over 100 similar maps covering cities all over the world. But a few years on, that is exactly what her Green Map System has done, by licensing for free a set of icons that designers anywhere can use to create their own local map. As well as promoting u'ban

sustainability, Green Maps offer a template for a system that can generate locally flavoured graphic information with a global connection.

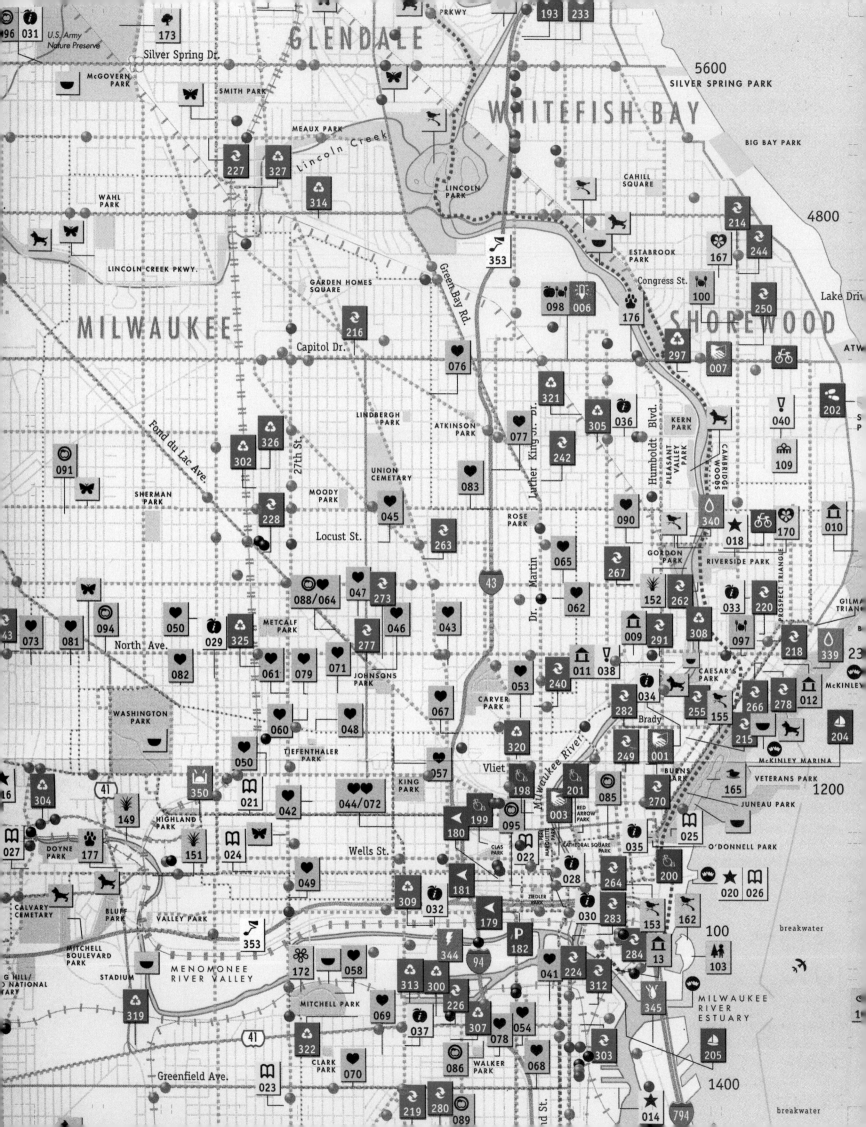

WORDS

WORDS

PIC0086   The Milwaukee Green Map

PIC0096   Green Map System Icons ~ www.greenmap.com

132

133

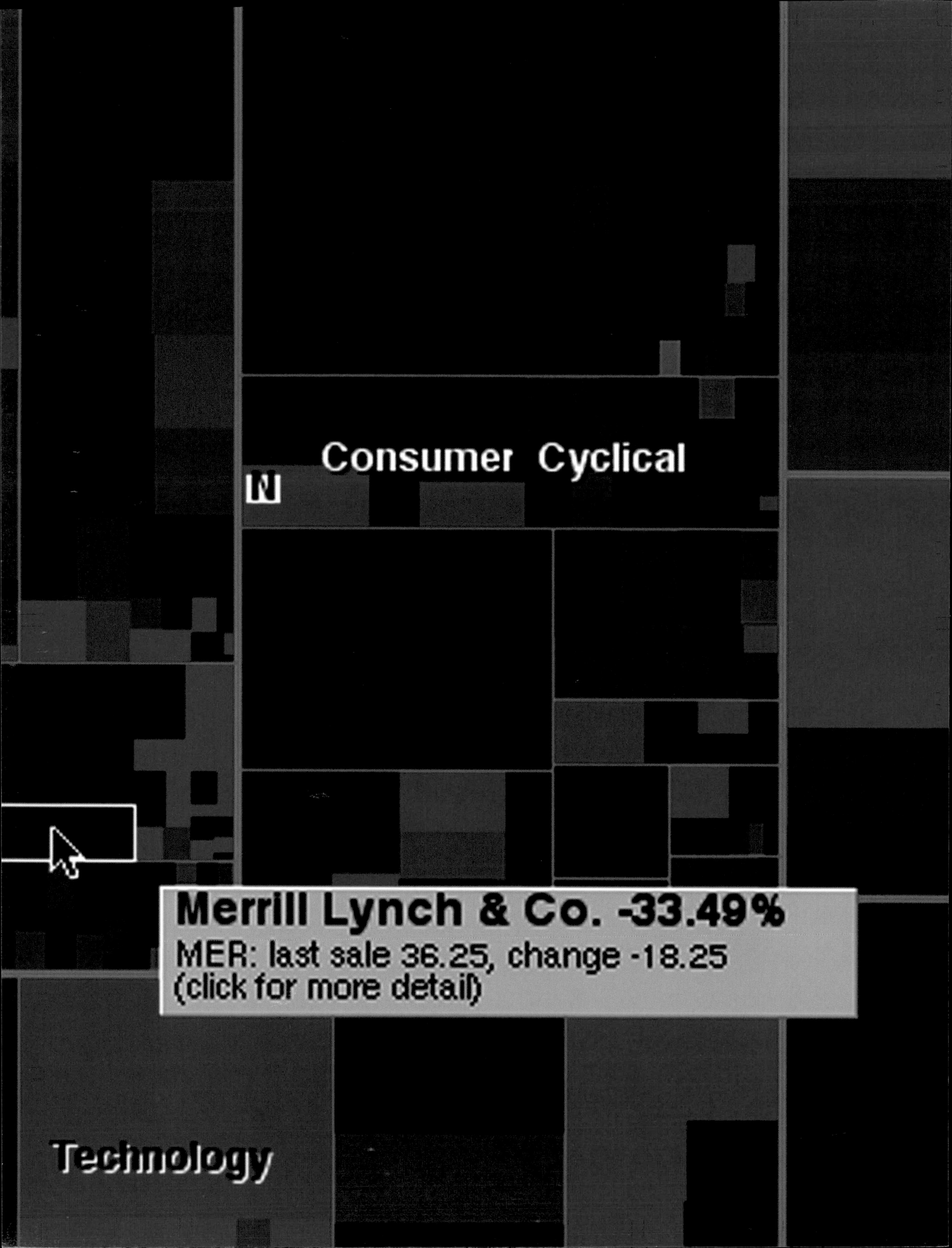
Consumer Cyclical
N
Merrill Lynch & Co. -33.49%
MER: last sale 36.25, change -18.25
(click for more detail)
Technology

Basic Materials

Technology

Telecom...

WORDS

SmartMoney.com

One of the breakthroughs in mainstream data visualization in recent years is the aerial photograph, or map approach, first put to stunning use by SmartMoney.com. Its Map of the Market offers a visual indication of the day's stock market performance of over 600 selected companies. Businesses are grouped by sector and each occupy an area - akin to a field or plot of land - that reflects its market capitalization. Its colour indicates how well the stock has performed in the day's trading: green = up, red = down. Reading the map as a whole

offers an immediate picture of the day's trading on the New York Stock Exchange, but it can also be 'drilled into' to find out more about specific areas of the market or about individual companies' news. SmartMoney also produces more detailed maps of individual sectors. There is no place to hide. As US voters demand greater accountability from their corporate leaders, this can be no bad thing.

PIC0097

Consumer Cyclical

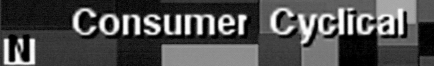

Merrill Lynch & Co. -12.61%
MER: last sale 36.25, change -5.23
(click for more detail)

Technology

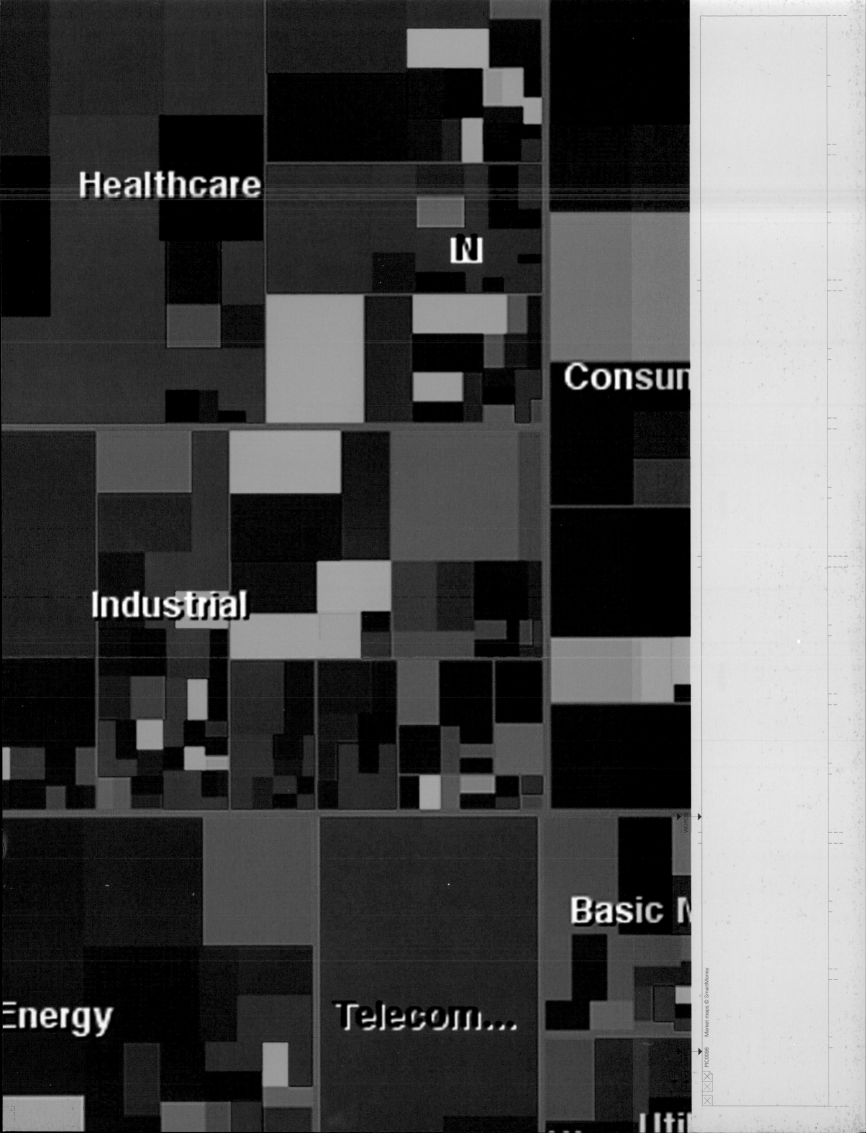

Pain assessment tool

Pictorial representations have been used to measure pain for many years. At the University Hospital Birmingham, however, the first ethnically sensitive pain assessment tool is helping patients in a strongly multicultural part of Britain express exactly how they are feeling to medical staff. It is overcoming problems associated with an inability to communicate one's pain, such as feelings of isolation and heightened pain. Available in five Asian languages - Punjabi, Gujarati, Urdu, Hindi and Bengali - the tool allows patients to indicate their level of pain on a scale from zero to three by pointing to one of four schematic faces.

WORDS

PIC00100 · Icon for people over pensionable age from chart in Design in Britain 2001 - 2002.
The Design Council

PIC0101 · Financial faces - Cranfield School of Management

WORDS

Financial faces

Directors of large businesses are trained to put on a brave face for the media in times of strife. This system of representing financial data with schematic faces offers a better way of getting at the truth. Developed by Professor Richard Taffler of Cranfield School of Management in the UK and Professor Malcolm Smith of the University of South Australia in Sydney, it proposes using the features of the face to convey an instant, telling picture of a company's financial health: eyebrow angle = liquidity; eye size = financial leverage; nose size = working

capital position; mouth angle = profitability. A changing expression over time tells its own story. The faces have been used internally by banks and investment firms, but their real value would be as a statutory feature of corporate annual reports, portraying information to shareholders in an accurate and accessible way - thereby putting paid to the overdesigned and misleading charts that have become such a feature of annual reports. Presently, the only businesses likely to use them publicly are those with a happy story to tell. More widely, the technique of representing data with smiley-style faces could be applied to almost any situation where several variables need to be conveyed simultaneously.

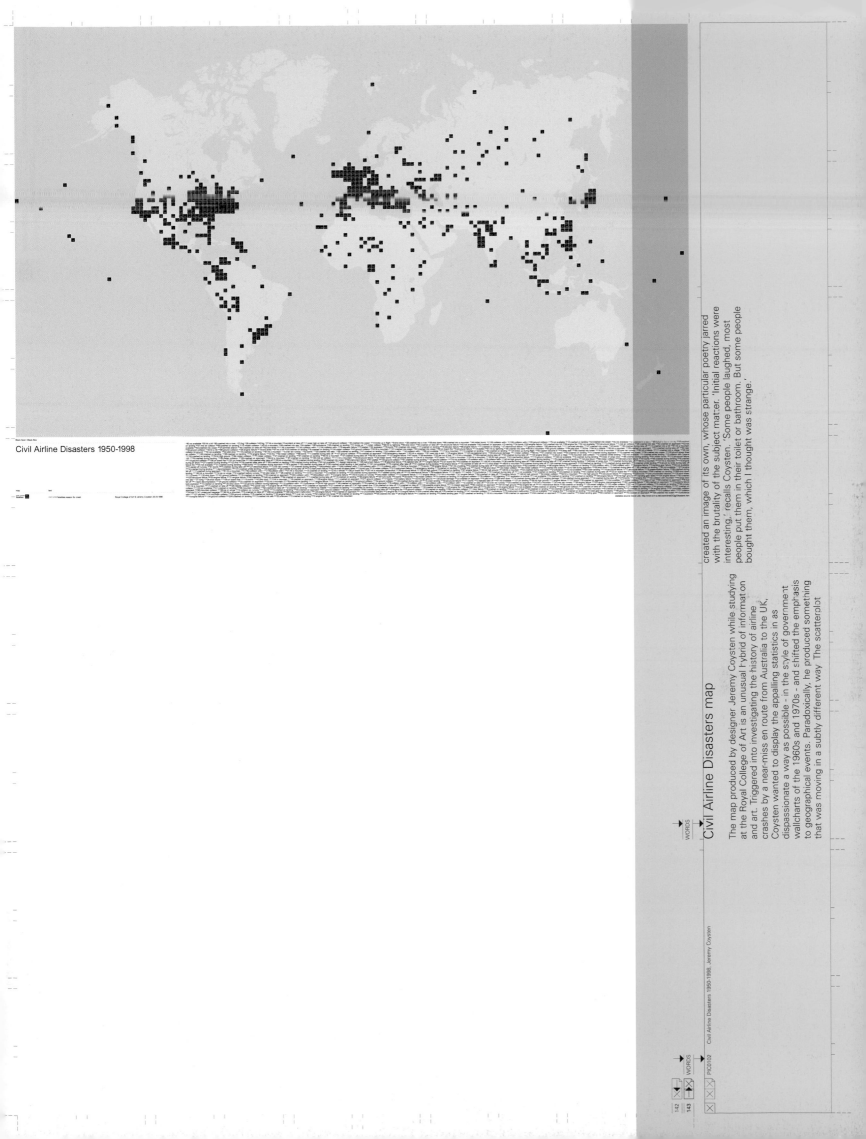

Civil Airline Disasters 1950-1998

WORDS

WORDS

Civil Airline Disasters 1950-1998, Jeremy Coysten

PIC0102

Civil Airline Disasters map

The map produced by designer Jeremy Coysten while studying at the Royal College of Art is an unusual hybrid of information and art. Triggered into investigating the history of airline crashes by a near-miss en route from Australia to the UK, Coysten wanted to display the appalling statistics in as dispassionate a way as possible - in the style of government wallcharts of the 1960s and 1970s - and shifted the emphasis to geographical events. Paradoxically, he produced something that was moving in a subtly different way. The scatterplot

created an image of its own, whose particular poetry jarred with the brutality of the subject matter. "Initial reactions were interesting," recalls Coysten. "Some people laughed, most people put them in their toilet or bathroom. But some people bought them, which I thought was strange."

56	X5966	96066	X6166	96266	X6366	96466	96566	96666	86766	86866	86966	87066	77166	87
55	95965	96065	96165	96265	96365	96465	86565	76665	76765	86865	86965	77065	67165	67
54	95964	96064	96164	96264	96364	96464	96564	86664	86764	86864	86964	87064	77164	77
53	X5963	96063	X6163	X6263	X6363	96463	96563	96663	96763	96863	86963	97063	97163	87
52	X5962	X6062	96162	96262	96362	96462	96562	96662	96762	96862	X6962	X7062	X7162	X7
51	95961	96061	X6161	96261	96361	96461	96561	96661	96761	X6861	96961	97061	X7161	X7
50	X5960	96060	X6160	96260	96360	96460	X6560	96660	96760	X6860	96960	X7060	X7160	X7
59	95959	X6059	X6159	X6259	X6359	X6459	X6559	96659	96759	X6859	X6959	X7059	97159	X7
58	X5958	96058	76158	76258	96358	X6458	X6558	X6658	X6758	X6858	X6958	87058	77158	X7
57	X5957	96057	56157	26257	66357	X6457	X6557	X6657	X6757	X6857	96957	57057	57157	97
56	85956	86056	46156	16256	46356	96456	X6556	X6656	X6756	X6856	76956	47056	57156	97
55	85955	86055	76155	56255	46355	66455	76555	86655	86755	76855	66955	57055	87155	97
54	95954	X6054	X6154	96254	86354	66454	66554	66654	66754	76854	86954	97054	97154	97
53	95953	86053	86153	86253	86353	76453	86553	86653	86753	86853	96953	97053	97153	97
52	65952	76052	86152	76252	66352	76452	86552	86652	86752	86852	86952	97052	X7152	87
51	25951	56051	76151	76251	66351	66451	66551	76651	86751	86851	76951	77051	87151	87
50	15950	36050	66150	66250	76350	66450	56550	66650	66750	76850	66950	77050	67150	47
49	25949	26049	26149	46249	66349	66449	56549	56649	46749	56849	56949	67049	57149	37

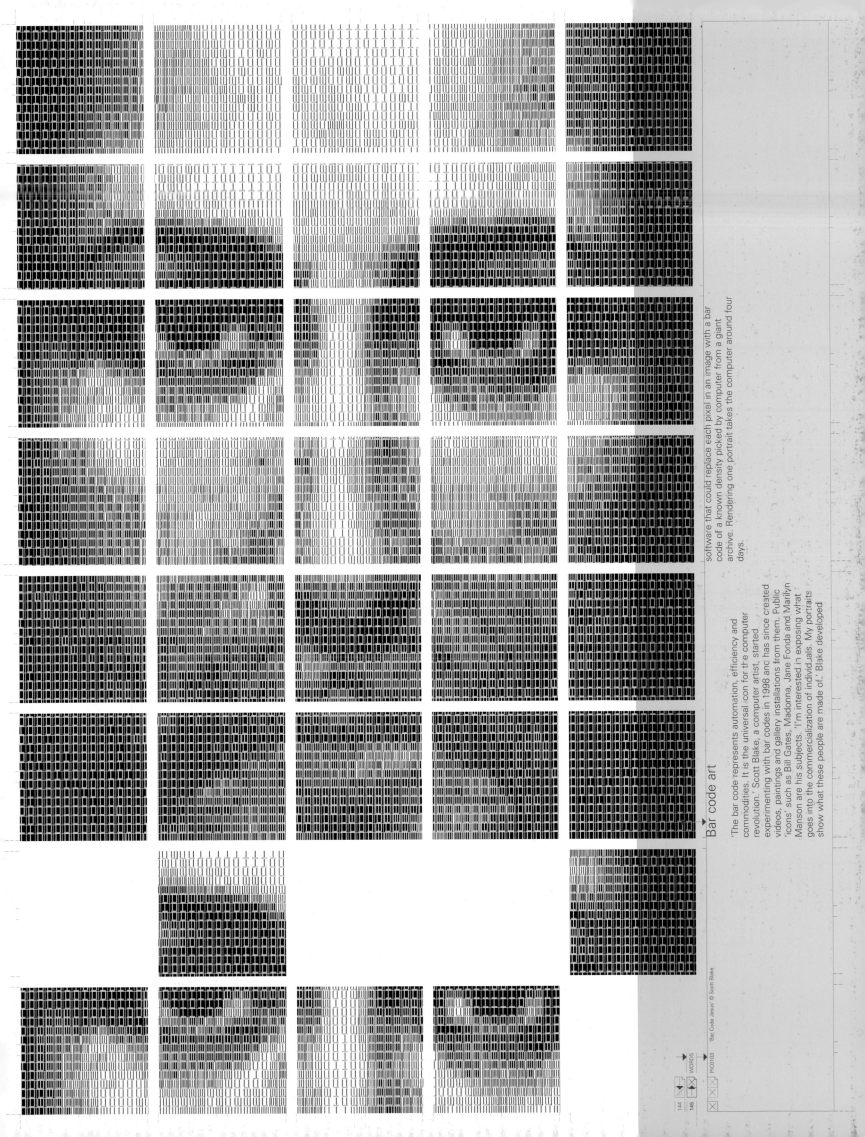

Bar code art

'The bar code represents automation, efficiency and commodities. It is the universal icon for the computer revolution.' Scott Blake, a computer artist, started experimenting with bar codes in 1998 and has since created videos, paintings and gallery installations from them. Public 'icons' such as Bill Gates, Madonna, Jane Fonda and Marilyn Manson are his subjects. 'I'm interested in exposing what goes into the commercialization of individuals. My portraits show what these people are made of.' Blake developed software that could replace each pixel in an image with a bar code of a known density picked by computer from a giant archive. Rendering one portrait takes the computer around four days.

WORDS

PICS

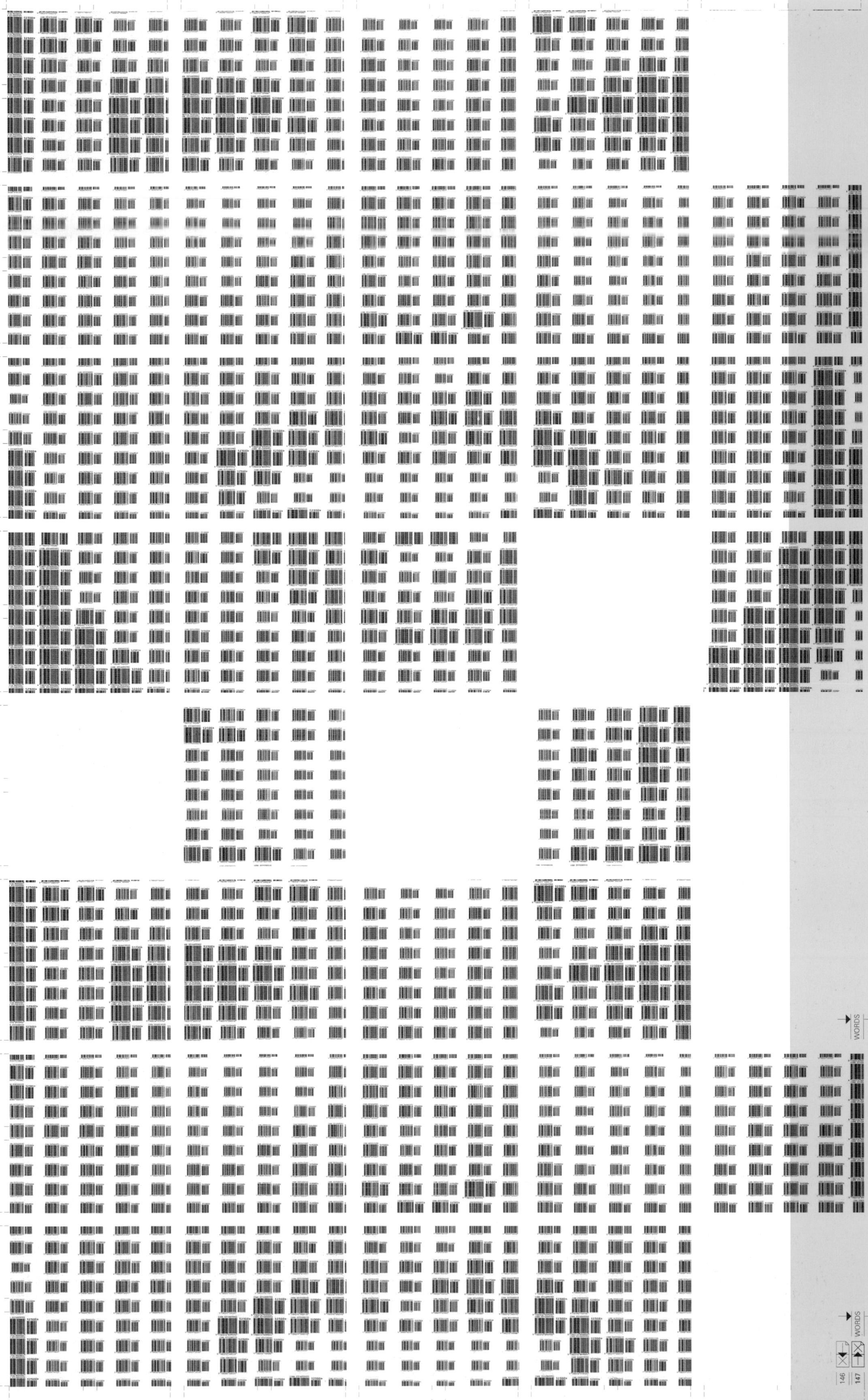

PIC0104

WORDS

WORDS

146
147

talk about specificity, what is simplistic and dead to talk about life'.

Pippo Lionni

The tableaux of all too human symbols created by Pippo Lionni in books and exhibitions offer a powerful critique of how saturation media coverage desensitizes us to real events. As well as exploring matters of life and death, they investigate the composition of matters of fact. At the same time, the flaws in our relationship with standard signs are exposed. "Pictograms are supposed to be self-evident," says Lionni. "This is the perversion of comfortable stereotype understanding. They use what is "without a doubt" to produce do,bt, the "universal" to

WORDS

WORDS PIC01105

All works by Pippo Lionni

from left to right
'Garden Party'- Agnes Costa collection, shown at the Brownstone Foundation, Paris, June 2001; 'Throwing Heads'- exhibition at La Cambre, Brussels, November 2001;
'Primetime - killme'- wall and video installation shown at Galerie Fréderic Giroux, June 2002; 'Schizoman'- wall installation, Galerie Franck Bordas, October 2001; Primetime - fuceme'- wall and video installation shown at Galerie Frédéric Giroux, June 2002; V-action - V choice' 'truth is exile' exhibition shown at the Brownstone Foundation, Paris, June 2001; 'Mindless and Saigon 1963'- wall installation shown at Galerie Frédéric Giroux, June 2002; 'in the name of g>d 1': wall installation shown at Galerie Frédéric Giroux, June 2002

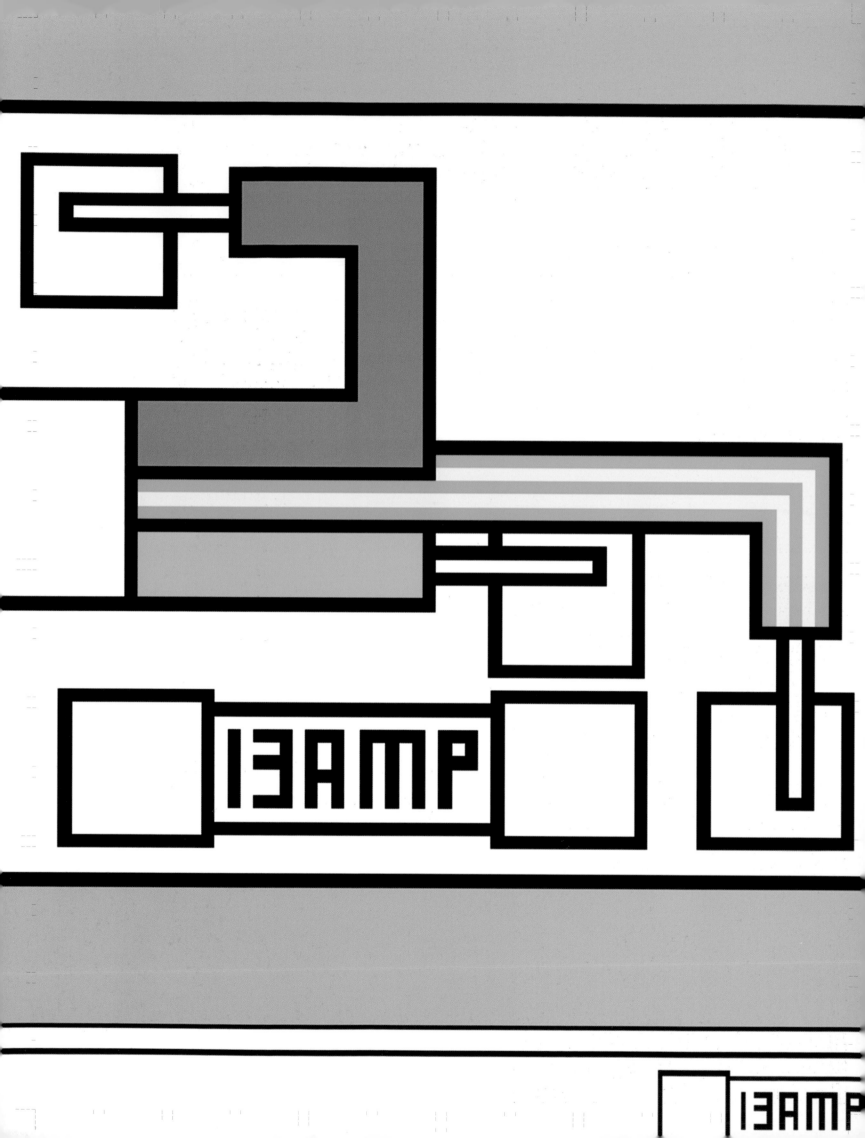

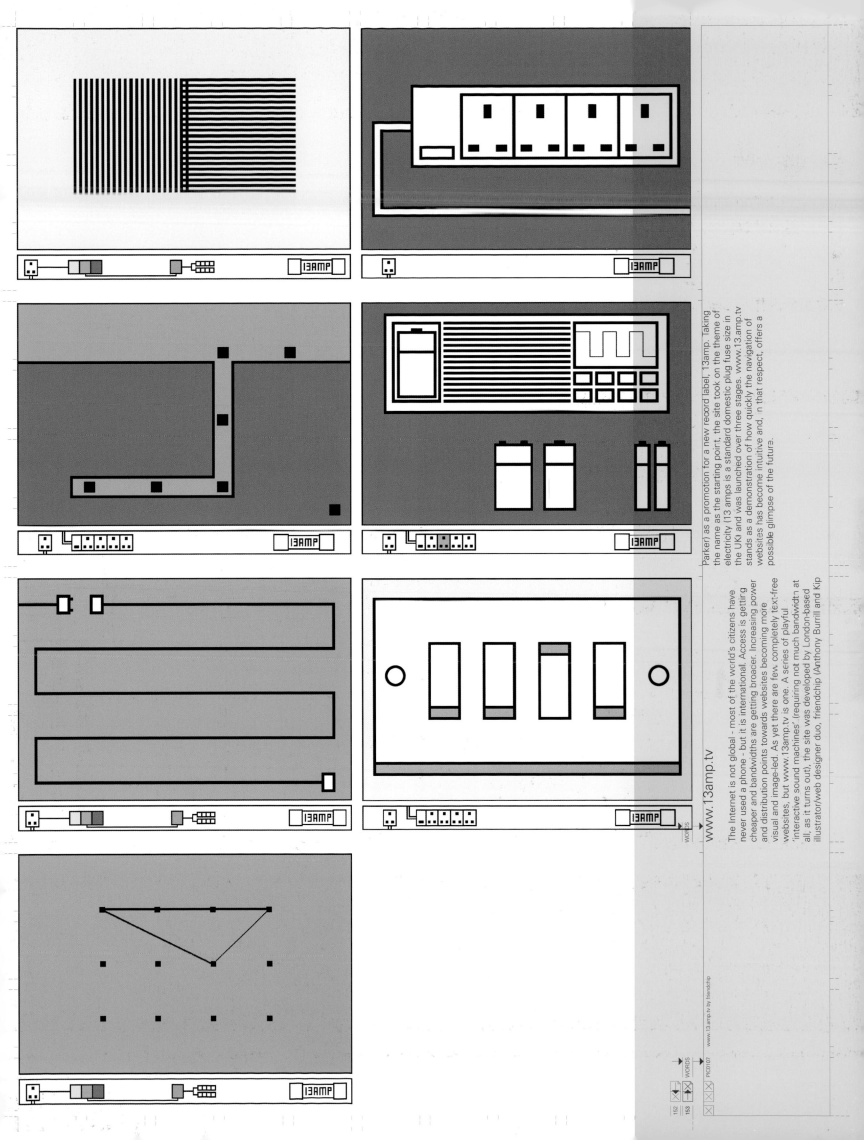

Parker) as a promotion for a new record label, 13amp. Taking the name as the starting point, the site took on the theme of electricity (13 amps is a standard domestic plug fuse size in the UK) and was launched over three stages. www.13.amp.tv stands as a demonstration of how quickly the navigation of websites has become intuitive and, in that respect, offers a possible glimpse of the future.

www.13amp.tv

The Internet is not global - most of the world's citizens have never used a phone - but it is international. Access is getting cheaper and bandwidths are getting broader. Increasing power and distribution points towards websites becoming more visual and image-led. As yet there are few completely text-free websites, but www.13amp.tv is one. A series of playful 'interactive sound machines' (requiring not much bandwidth at all, as it turns out), the site was developed by London-based illustrator/web designer duo, friendchip (Anthony Burrill and Kip

www.13.amp.tv by friendchip

WORDS
WORDS
PICN107   www.13.amp.tv

152
153

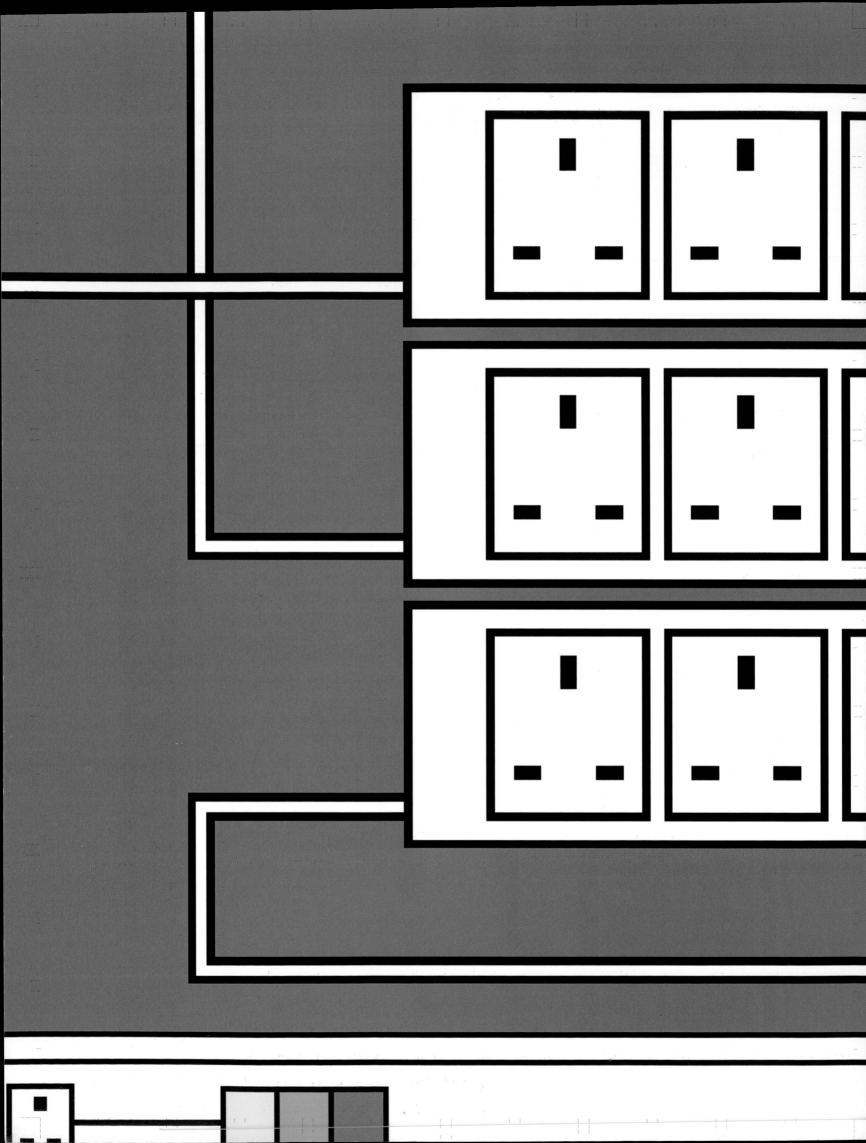

PIC0109   Escaped Animals by Julian Opie outside Tate Modern, London
(photos: Michael Evamy)

WORDS

Escaped Animals

Julian Opie, one of the celebrated 'New British Artists', is another who finds inspiration in the graphic flotsam and jetsam of modern life: 'public places where languages take a form such as signs, gravestones, banners, pop-ups.' Opie produced a series of 13 road signs, each featuring a small animal, as part of the opening programme for the Baltic Centre for Contemporary Art in Gateshead. However, these 'Escaped Animals' acted as a surreptitious ad campaign for the Baltic. In the style of recent billboard ads which, by using only

ambiguous imagery, convey an element of mystery and exclusivity to attract attention, the signs drew the curiosity of art lovers around the UK. Throughout the summer of 2002 they were clustered in slightly chaotic groups outside other major art venues, as if they'd lost their bearings: "This isn't the right place; which way to the Baltic?' By being lost,, they pointed the way.

Colors 13

'The first ever magazine without words' was how corporate sponsor Benetton described the 13th edition of its controversial magazine, Colors, in December 1995. An attempt by founding editor-in-chief and art director Tibor Kalman to create a publication that could be enjoyed equally by anyone, in any country, Colors 13 used a barrage of powerfully juxtaposed photo library stock to explore global issues at a human level. The principle that images, rather than words, will command the widest - and largest - audience, is now an accepted rule of magazine publishing and is being followed by high- and lowbrow publications. Now part of modern design iconography, Colors 13 was Kalman's last issue in charge. He died in 1999.

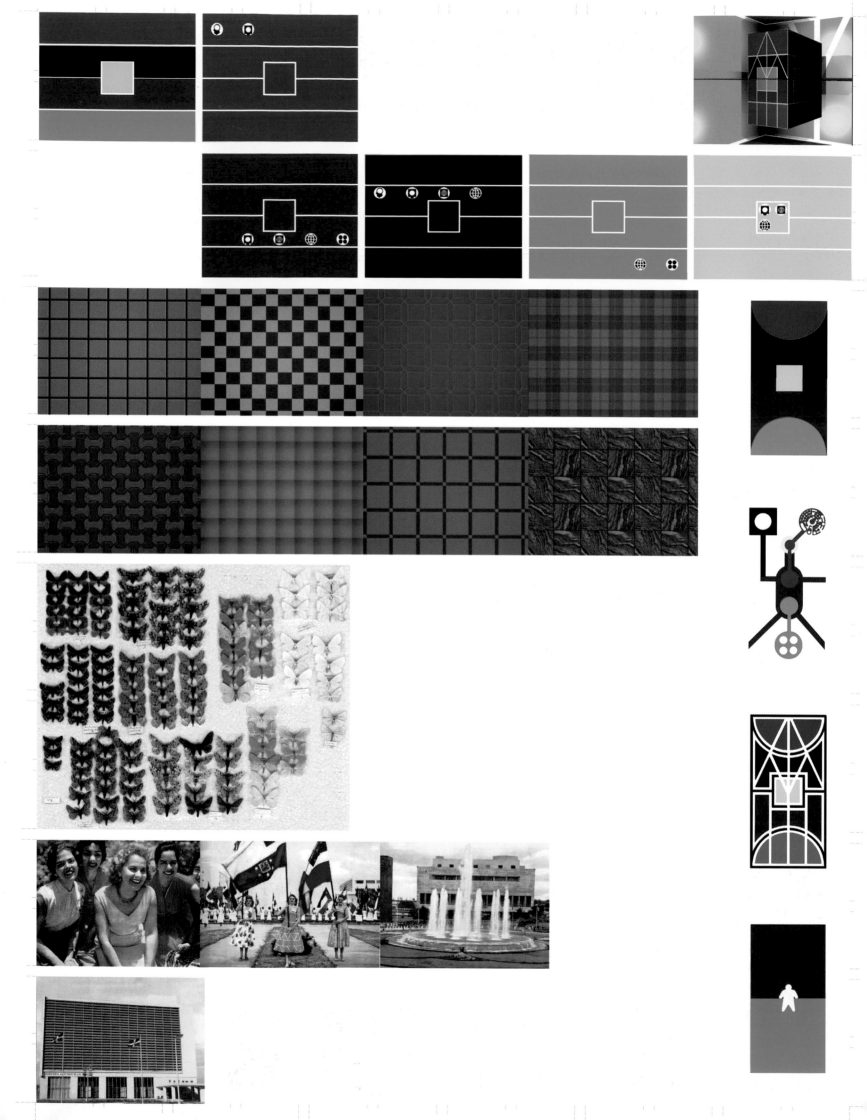

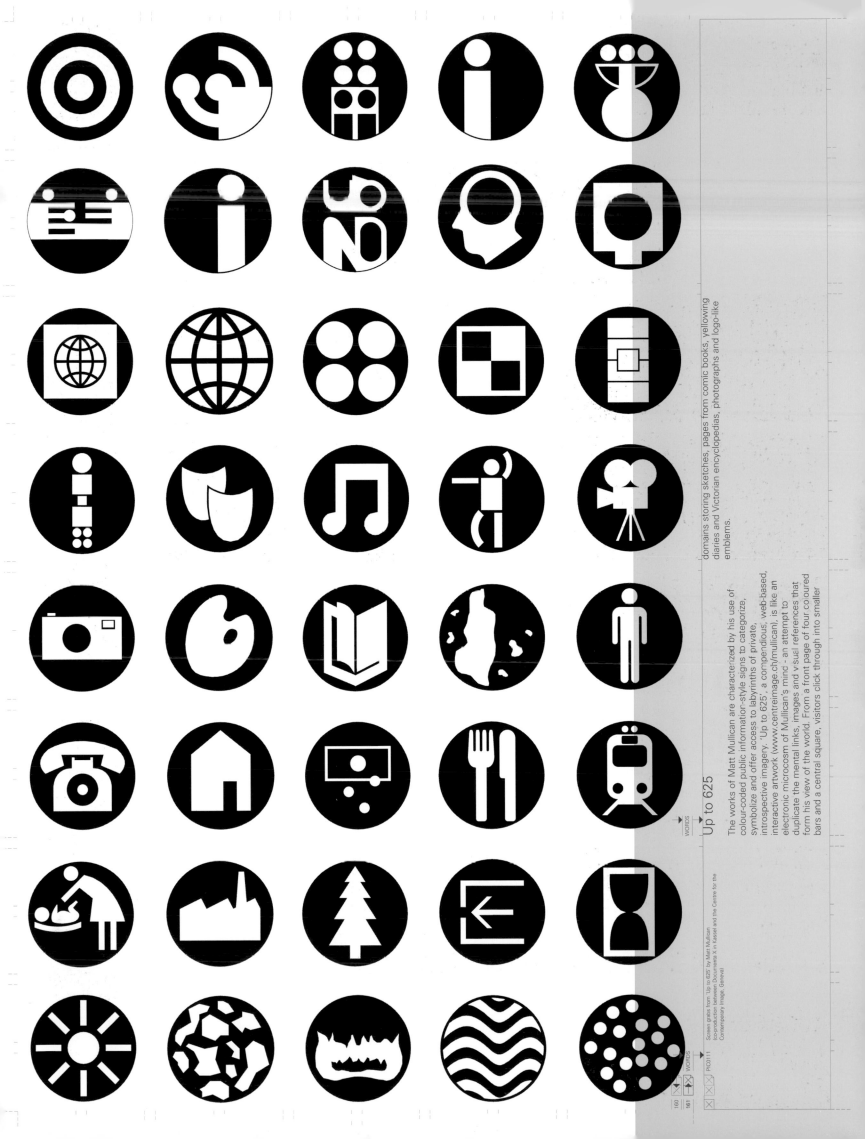

domains storing sketches, pages from comic books, yellowing diaries and Victorian encyclopedias, photographs and logo-like emblems.

Up to 625

The works of Matt Mullican are characterized by his use of colour-coded public information-style signs to categorize, symbolize and offer access to labyrinths of private, introspective imagery. 'Up to 625', a compendious, web-based, interactive artwork (www.centreimage.ch/mullican), is like an electronic microcosm of Mullican's mind - an attempt to duplicate the mental links, images and visual references that form his view of the world. From a front page of four coloured bars and a central square, visitors click through into smaller

Screen grab from 'Up to 625' by Matt Mullican (co-production between Documenta X in Kassel and the Centre for the Contemporary Image, Geneva)

WORDS
PIC0111
WORDS

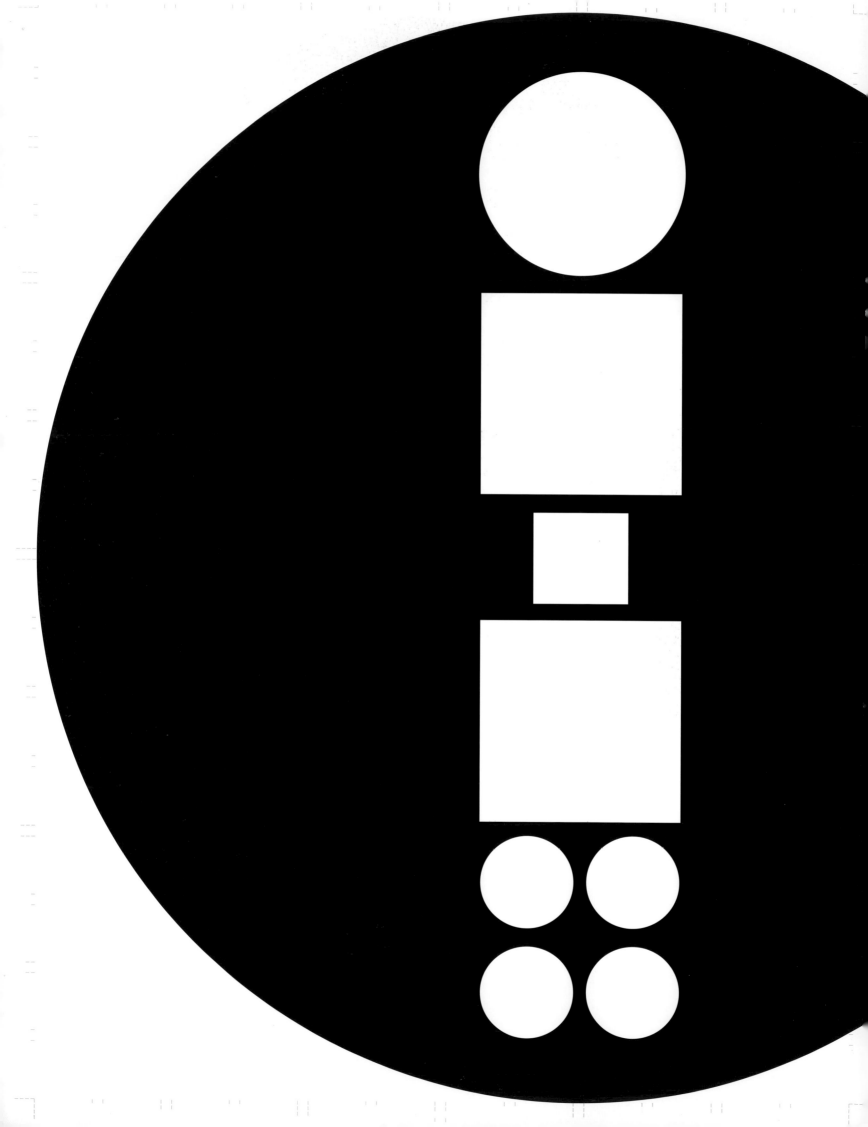

WORDS

WORDS

PIC0112   Pictograms from 'Up to 625' by Matt Mullican
(co-production between Documenta X in Kassel and the Centre for the
Contemporary Image, Geneva)

Blobs

Fairies

Changed priorities ahead

Mischief rather than subversion was behind the deviant warning signs that appeared in Exeter, south-west England on the morning of 31 August 2000. A local group of artists calling themselves the Interdimensional Pixie Broadcast Network claimed to have initially produced the signs for their own amusement, but then started to consider the relationship between road-users and road signs. 'We're "hacking" an infrastructure of symbol/response which operates between the authorities and the public,' claimed the group. Irresponsible?

Dangerous? The IPBN argues not, since none of the symbols chosen could be mistaken for important warnings about the behaviour of the road ahead, e.g. a sharp bend or fork in the road. 'If (drivers) see an image of a snail it might actually cross their minds to be more aware of snails. Or to slow down a bit, which wouldn't be a bad thing.' The local police force did not agree, and made sure the signs were removed by sunset.

WORDS
PIC0113   Digital shots around Exeter, south-west England
by International Pixie Broadcast Network

164
165